THE EXECUTOR'S CHALLENGE

First edition published in 2024 by
Porcupine Press
PO Box 2756
Pinegowrie, 2123
South Africa
dgrwrite@iafrica.com
ISBN 978-1-9284-5597-4

Cover design and text layout by wim@wimrheeder.co.za
Set in 11 point on 16 point, Cambria
Printed and bound by Creda Communications (Pty) Ltd, Cape Town

DECEASED ESTATES

THE EXECUTOR'S CHALLENGE

FOR EVERYONE

THE ALTERNATIVE TO A DISCRETIONARY LIVING TRUST

MERVIN MESSIAS

PORCUPINE PRESS

Johannesburg

IMPORTANT NOTE

This publication is intended as a general guide only and does not constitute professional advice. The information, opinions and ideas which it contains are the author's and not intended to be a comprehensive study, or to provide legal advice, and should not be treated as a substitute for legal advice concerning particular situations. If the reader requires personal assistance or advice, a competent professional should be consulted before taking any action based on the information provided.

It is intended to provide helpful and informative material on the subject matter covered and is sold with the understanding that the author and publisher are not engaged in rendering professional services in this book.

For information, the author may be contacted at the following address:

Mervin Messias: BA, LLB (Wits) / TEP
(Trust and Estate Practitioner)
Address: 104, 11th Street, Parkmore,
Sandton 2196, South Africa
Contact: +27 11 783 0108
Email: mervin@mmtrustspecialist.co.za
Website: www.mmtrustspecialist.co.za

CONTENTS

ABOUT THE AUTHOR

Trust and Estate Practitioner Mervin Messias has been a practising attorney for more than 40 years. The wealth of knowledge he has amassed across a broad range of legal disciplines has been skilfully channelled into developing a Trust and Deceased Estates business.

His experience and reputation as a Trust and Deceased Estate Practitioner are recognised both nationally and internationally and he is renowned for his extraordinary depth of knowledge and proficiency in both legal disciplines.

Over the more than 40-year period, he has dealt with the challenges faced by executors preparing for and winding up deceased estates. These matters motivated him to write this book. It has practical relevance to the testator, his or her loved ones, and the executor.

In South Africa he has obtained BA LLB degrees from the University of the Witwatersrand, been a member of The South African Law Society Trusts and Estates committee, and a member of The Society of Trust and Estate Practitioners (STEP), where he served as chairperson of the Johannesburg branch for twelve consecutive years. He has also been a member of The South African Institute of Tax Practitioners (SAIT), which recognised him as a Master Tax Practitioner, and a member of The Fiduciary Institute of Southern

Africa (FISA). He has lectured to and trained Attorneys, Accountants and Financial Advisors, and given numerous presentations to members of the public.

Internationally, he has been admitted as a Solicitor in England and Wales, Australia and New Zealand, as an Attorney in Lesotho, and as a member of the National Network of Estate Planning Attorneys of the United States of America. He has also been admitted, by invitation, as an Academician of the International Academy of Estate and Trust Law.

In Addition, Mervin Messias has been awarded "Best Lawyers for Trusts and Estates" from 2009–2024, consecutively.

His passion for preparedness and simplifying complex legal concepts to make them accessible to more people inspired him to author his first book, *Estate Planning Trusts for Everyone – Discretionary Living Trusts – A Legacy for Generations*. It is a condensed and easy read for anyone wanting to understand the role and advantages of living trusts within a comprehensive, multi-generational estate plan.

FOREWORD

This is a user-friendly book which endeavours to unravel the complex task of winding up a deceased estate by an executor in South Africa.

The book is also designed to advise the general public on how to prepare a person who is to be nominated as the executor or an appropriately qualified agent. It is a step-by-step guide to provide material and meaningful assistance to the executor to facilitate ease of administration of a deceased estate and the efficient completion thereof in accordance with South African law.

A nominated executor may not be adequately informed about the process and the scope of work. Compliance, administrative detail, practical application and knowing how to manage the expectations of a deceased's loved ones are all essential elements that have been included.

The book endeavours to explain and cover the necessary steps required to wind up a deceased estate.

I commend Mervin Messias for the writing of this book. I have no hesitation in recommending it.

HUSSAN GOGA
Attorney, Notary Public and Conveyancer
Chairperson of the Law Society of South Africa Committee on Deceased Estates, Trusts, and Planning.

ACKNOWLEDGEMENTS

This book is dedicated to my three daughters – Lauren, Cara, and Jade – who continue to bring me joy, inspiration, and pride, to my wonderful sons-in-law Adam and Shmuel, and my grandchildren.

In appreciation, I should like to acknowledge the expertise of the following individuals who assisted to develop, write, and bring this book to fruition.

Assistance with research and written content:
Sandra Cormie, DipEd (TTC)

Assistance with artwork and technical support:
Najeedah Dawood.

Editing of the law:
Hussan Goga. Attorney, Notary Public and Conveyancer, Chairperson of the Law Society of South Africa Committee on Deceased Estates, Trusts, and Planning.

Tax advice:
Advocate Anthony (Tony) Harding Davey. BA (Natal), LLB (Natal), LLM (Unisa), H Dip Tax (Wits), Post Grad Dip Int Tax (UJ), Chartered Tax Adviser (SAIT), Fellow of the Institute of Chartered Secretaries, Advocate of the High Court.

PREFACE

This book is intended to jolt the living into getting their affairs in order, since no one should be expected to wind up a chaotic deceased estate. It is presented as an overview of what is required to wind up a deceased estate in South Africa and is relevant to testators, testatrices and executors.

When the process of winding up a deceased estate is explained, the testator/testatrix ought to grasp the full extent and complexity of the work involved for the executor. Understanding the intricacies may come as a shock, but greater clarity now will facilitate the preparation they need to undertake in support of the administrative process after they die. Thorough preparation will not only assist the executor, but it should also ease the burden on those counting on this person for immediate and long-term financial provision.

While the executor can only proceed at the pace determined by the preparation, the prevailing situation at the Master's office should also be taken into account. Make sure that you obtain a stamp of receipt on copies of all documents lodged at the Master's office.

Making provision for debt is a fundamental consideration in any estate plan. Debt could land any family in dire straits, as the law prioritises settling creditor debt ahead of paying heirs. An untimely death, a mountain of debt and no estate plan may very well leave a family with a few scraps, or nothing at all. My chapter on Life Insurance (chapter 20) explains the merits of having a plan that provides for immediate liquidity after death.

The information about the estate made available by the testator will also help the nominated executor make a more informed decision before accepting or declining the nomination. Thereafter, it will serve as a useful consultative guide.

All deceased estates are governed by the Administration of Estates Act 66 of 1965 – every executor should print a copy and keep it handy. Go to www.justice.gov.za/legislation/acts/1965. Regardless of value, all deceased estates must be wound up according to the provisions of the Act.

A Will specifies how you would like your personal and/or business assets disposed of after death, stipulates which assets should be distributed to whom, and nominates an executor to complete the administration of your estate and effect the distributions. Without a Will, the Master of the High Court will appoint an executor and the assets belonging to your deceased estate will be distributed according to the rules of intestate succession (a predetermined order of relatives). The recipients may not be the people you had in mind.

When you die, the nominee executor who accepts the appointment has first to be authorised by the Master of the High Court. This requires the nominee to file prescribed documents with the Master before the

Letters of Executorship can be issued. The Letters will give the executor access to all the relevant personal and business information required to wind up your estate. A pre-prepared dossier of key information would be a great time-saver!

Like any new undertaking, executorship has its rewards and pitfalls. Make time to discuss the nomination with your nominee ahead of time. To thrust executorship, without warning, on someone who is inexperienced and possibly dealing with grief themselves, is unreasonable. You will have missed a golden opportunity to discuss the rationale behind the contents of your Will, which the executor may find useful when sensitive matters require attention.

When an executor understands your thinking and planning, it facilitates the interaction with your family and heirs and guides any decision-making that may be required of him or her.

1.
THE ROLE AND SIGNIFICANCE OF A WILL

A Will is not mandatory according to South African law, but it is suggested that anyone with assets creates one.

According to the Wills Act 7 of 1953, every person of the age of 16 years or more may make a Will unless, at the time of making the Will, they are mentally incapable of appreciating the nature and effect of their actions.

To be valid, a Will must be in writing (hand, typed or printed). The formalities required in the execution of a Will are covered in the Wills Act, which can be accessed online from the Department of Justice and Constitutional Development website. Any oversight may bring the authenticity of the Will into question and open the door to litigation, a costly exercise to the estate and interfamily relationships.

When nominating an executor in a Will, you should:

- Ask yourself whether the person you wish to nominate is *fit for the task* – suitable in terms of age, skills, reputation, reliability, availability, and geographic location.

- *Discuss it with the nominee* and make sure he/she *has agreed to undertake the task.*
- Establish a relationship with the person ahead of time, provide updates on any changes and prep him/her thoroughly so that when the time comes, the process can be completed more efficiently.
- Ensure the nominee knows where your Will and supporting documents may be found.

A poorly drafted Will has the propensity to cause the mother of all headaches for both the executor and your beneficiaries. The slightest ambiguity could trigger delays and costly legal consequences.

If you already have a Will, check that it is in order and address any potential problems timeously. Make every effort to avoid saddling your executor with difficulties before he/she has even left the starting blocks.

The three essential components to a Will are:

- *The revocation clause.* Since the creation of a Will *does not automatically override any previous Will/s or codicil/s,* the revocation clause is crucial to legally cancel any previous Will/s or codicil/s that may still be in existence, often long forgotten. Otherwise, when you die, any previous Will/s that come to light could be used to challenge your most recent Will and result in litigation. Should you own assets in other countries and sign separate Wills for each country, care should be taken to ensure that the revocation clause in each Will does not affect all other Wills.
- *The nomination of an executor.*

- The *disposition of the estate*, which refers to the disposal and transfer of property to beneficiaries as determined by you in your Will. The choice for every individual who has assets is simple – either their assets will be distributed as they intended by way of a valid Will, or the Intestate Succession Act 81 of 1987 will decide for them. Your hard-earned legacy could end up in the most undeserving hands.

Your Will may also include your final wishes regarding your funeral arrangements and remains. Perhaps you have a funeral policy or specific personal requests that relate to your funeral and final resting place. Avoid family conflict and express these in your Will.

A Will requires care, forethought, and planning. It should make proper provision for diverse contingencies, generally unimagined by a layperson.

When creating a Will, South African law allows for freedom of testation, a liberty whereby you may include (or exclude) *almost* whomever you like. The parameters are defined by the Constitution and various Acts of Parliament.

Those who signed as witnesses to your Will (and their respective spouses) are, subject to certain exceptions, disqualified and may not receive any benefit from your Will.

A specific person may legally be excluded from a Will by adding a Deliberate Exclusion clause when drawing it up, or later by codicil.

Certain countries have laws that protect heirs with

mandatory succession rights (known as primogeniture, the right of succession belonging to the first-born child or eldest son). This has been declared unconstitutional and invalid in South Africa. It was found to be discriminatory against women, and children born out of wedlock.

Many people need help to fully understand why a Will should be regarded as a priority. Consider this: *no one knows when they are going to die*. The cruel reality is that disease and accidents strike randomly.

If you die without a Will, you will be regarded as having died intestate. In such event, the Master must first receive nominations from beneficiaries for the appointment of an executor before making such appointment. Those who are still alive will inherit in the following manner. The surviving spouse will be entitled to a one-half share of the joint estate if your marriage is in community of property. The surviving spouse will also be the sole heir if there are no descendants, or if the value of the deceased estate does not exceed R250 000,00. If the value of the deceased estate exceeds R250 000,00 the surviving spouse and descendants will benefit and, in their absence, siblings. Descendants include pre-deceased children leaving issue, adopted children and those born out of wedlock. (For more detail, refer to The Intestate Succession Act 81 of 1987. It describes how the provisions are governed by other Acts as well as how customary marriage laws are accommodated, the order of precedence in the receipt of benefits according to marriage and bloodline, and how the estate should be shared.)

Failing to make a Will may open the inheritance door to the most undeserving.

A Will can only be contested on the grounds of validity or terms. Examples include a lack of testamentary capacity (again, your mental competence to create and sign a Will), a failure to meet the necessary legal formalities (such as stipulated in the Wills Act 7 of 1953) required in the creation of a valid Will, claims of forgery, undue influence, or the presentation of other Wills, all of which will have to be proven in a court of law. This will stall the process and incur legal costs.

Joint Wills are invariably cumbersome and difficult to interpret with any certainty and may incur unwelcome consequences associated with the massing of two estates. Separate Wills are highly recommended and less likely to cause disputes.

Consulting a specialist offers you the perfect opportunity to ask questions and solicit constructive advice. It is very important to fully understand the contents and conditions of your Will *before* signing it. For instance, what do "gifts" (legacies) constitute and how is one "gift" different from another? A specialist should explain things in layman's language.

- A specific gift may be a specific item like "the oil painting by X".
- A non-specific gift may be "all my personal possess-ions".
- A non-residuary gift, like "R500 000 to the executor to put in trust for a disabled child".
- A residual gift is what is left over after specific gifts

(including financial gifts) have been distributed, and all expenses and taxes have been paid.

When constructing your Will, establish what should happen to a gift/legacy willed to a beneficiary in the event he or she predeceases you. A survivorship clause would be the most pragmatic solution.

Also, avoid downloading a generic Will template off the internet because you have no way of knowing if it complies with the South African laws listed below and if not, what the impact might be.

- *Wills Act 7 of 1953*
- *Intestate Succession Act 81 of 1987*
- *Maintenance of Surviving Spouses Act 27 of 1990*
- *Matrimonial Property Act 88 of 1984*
- *Insolvency Act 24 of 1936*
- *Trust Property Control Act 57 of 1988*
- *Estate Duty Act 45 of 1955*
- *Administration of Estates Act 66 of 1965.*

The detail and precision are crucial to the interpretation and execution, especially if contested after you die. The levels of incompetence and ignorance made evident in poorly drafted Wills are inclined to test the patience of presiding judges and visit the most regrettable fallout on beneficiaries.

The efficiency of a Will's execution depends entirely on the quality of its construction.

Here are a few random points to consider regarding a Will:

- The Master requires the original signed Will. If the Will of any deceased person is not in the Republic, the Master may accept a copy certified by a competent public authority in the country in which the Will is. The Master may also accept a certified copy of the Will if it is also the Will of any other deceased person and has been registered and accepted by any other Master. In all other cases, the Master requires the original Will to be submitted for registration and acceptance and a certified copy is not acceptable without a court order, so the onus is on you to ensure that your Will is stored in a safe place.

- Any signed codicil forms part of the Will and must be submitted to the Master with the Will.

- In the absence of a formal Will, any documents purporting to be a Will must be submitted to the Master. If there is more than one, the Master will decide which one may be relevant, usually by date.

- Electronic Wills require a court order to be accepted as valid.

- In the case of a joint Will created by a couple, when one spouse dies, the surviving spouse is advised to draw up a new Will. Elements of the original joint Will may no longer apply.

- If a testator dies within three months of being granted a final order of divorce or annulment, unless he or she has amended the Will to express a contrary intention, the law will revert to the Will prior to the dissolution of the marriage. Wills must be updated as soon as there are significant family changes – like death (of a beneficiary), marriage, divorce, or births.

- If the Will has been drawn up in any language other than one of the eleven official languages of South Africa (Ndebele, Northern Sotho, Sotho, SiSwati, Tsonga, Venda, Xhosa, Zulu, Tswana, English or Afrikaans), a sworn translation into English or Afrikaans should be lodged with the Master.
- While the testator has the right to exempt the executor from providing a Bond of Security to perform his function, the Master will usually insist that the executor furnish a bond of security or alternatively, be assisted by an attorney.

Property that falls OUTSIDE a Will includes any property where the deceased named a beneficiary – such as, life insurance proceeds, property held in a trust or retirement funds.

MAIN POINTS:
- Have your Will drawn up professionally.
- Keep your affairs in order.
- Inform your executor of any changes.

2.
IS YOUR NOMINATED EXECUTOR UP TO THE TASK?

There are no shortcuts to winding up an estate. An executor's task is completed only when all the administrative procedures have been finalised in accordance with the Administration of Estates Act 66 of 1965.

The ideal executor will be responsible, persistent and administratively competent. Some business acumen would be an advantage, particularly if businesses, complex investment portfolios and multiple properties form part of your estate.

DEFINITION AND DUTIES

First, the executor must apply to the Master of the High Court for Letters of Executorship. The Master may require security in the form of an executor's bond, and will inspect the Will to check for any applicable exemptions before issuing the Letters of Executorship. Those automatically exempted from the obligation to furnish security are a surviving spouse, parent, or child of the deceased.

The Letters give the executor authority to access

all the information that will be required to wind up your estate – from bank statements, insurance policies and share portfolios to vehicle finance agreements, tax returns, business agreements, and so on.

The Letters of Executorship also give the executor authority to call on specialists for help – like attorneys and accountants. Unless a deceased person's Will makes specific provision for the specialist costs that may be required to wind up the estate (which, if used, must then reflect in the Liquidation and Distribution account), the fee for any such external services must be negotiated and paid from the executor's fees. The current recommended fee is 3.5% of the gross value of the assets in the estate (VAT is applied if the executor is a registered VAT vendor) plus 6% on income accrued and collected after death.

Acceptance of the appointment is a formal acknowledgement that the executor will protect the assets of the estate to the best of his or her ability and take full responsibility for them during the process. Accepting financial liability for the estate is a serious undertaking. Any losses in value incurred by the executor may require restitution from his/her own pocket. Opportunities for negligent, irregular, or reckless administration and mischief exist, but the Master also has the authority to remove an executor for improper administration or loss to the estate.

Once he/she has the Letters, the executor must locate, collate, and account for every item you owned (assets) and owed (liabilities) as at your *date of death*.

It is important to consider the emotional toll the

executor may face, especially if he/she is close to you. Will he/she be able to manage personal grief without allowing it to affect judgement and proficiency?

THE ATTRIBUTES NECESSARY FOR EXECUTORSHIP

Money can bring out the worst in people. Family bonds are often tested when money is involved, and difficult heirs sometimes feel a sense of entitlement to a greater share of the estate. The executor should not allow him/herself to be manipulated or intimidated by family, especially if asked to act contrary to the provisions of your Will.

Ponder these points and check whether the nominee fits the profile comfortably. Is he/she:

- Able to stay focused and separate emotional issues from responsibilities?
- Able to remain impartial in his/her line of duty?
- Logical and able to follow a process step-by-step?
- Well organised, systems-orientated, and able to adhere to time frames?
- Skilled at handling financial matters and keeping detailed records?
- A good communicator who can openly and honestly answer questions from heirs?
- Able to withstand intimidation, since accepting the role may put him/her in conflict with your heirs?
- Equipped to handle family grudges that may resurface after many years of being ignored? These will have to be skilfully and impartially managed to over-

come the obstacles and get the task done.

- Easily intimidated by meddlesome extended family? Outspoken in-laws may get underfoot and express what they believe to be right and equitable, but it may not be what the Will says!
- Competent to provide regular status reports to heirs?
- Able to defend any impending litigation regarding the estate?
- Experiencing any health issues that could negatively impact performance as executor?
- Geographically suited to the task? The Administration of Estates Act requires that your death must be reported within 14 (fourteen) days to the jurisdiction in which you died and had been ordinarily resident for the last 12 months. It may be that your assets are situated elsewhere.

Typical questions the executor may have to answer:
Why is it taking so long? When can I expect to receive my money? Can I claim some of it now? The Will does not mention X, may I take it now? Why don't you leave X, Y and Z out of the inventory so we can take them now? How much are you getting paid? Why won't you reduce (or waive) your fee?

Focus is key. When faced with emotional issues, he/she cannot allow heirs or other meddlesome parties to obstruct or influence decision making. He/she must act according to your Will. The heirs, however, are entitled to enter into a Redistribution Agreement if they consider it expedient to do so, subject to any equalisation of values, if applicable.

Executorship is not for the faint-hearted. It is a complex process that requires a systematic approach and a whole lot of fortitude!

MAIN POINT:

- Choose your executor carefully.

3.
HOW THE TESTATOR CAN ASSIST THE EXECUTOR

A good proportion of the responsibility for the smooth execution of your Will and administration of your estate rests with you.

Wills are often influenced by relationships and family dynamics, so that what is fair and what is deserved becomes a debate of conscience. No executor wants to step into a war zone precipitated by the terms of a Will. For multiple reasons these issues are best settled while you are alive – because if the Will is challenged in court, the cost to your family and the estate could be incalculable.

The South African constitution allows for freedom of testation with very few limitations. To avoid falling foul of the law or dissent in your family, seek specialist advice.

Once you have approached the person to act as your executor and he/she has agreed, preparedness and communication between you ahead of time will allow him/her to step up to the plate, take control of the situation and access all the documents needed to make a start so that your family is free to grieve.

STEP 1 FOR THE TESTATOR

Consider telling your heirs how your estate is to be shared and why it is structured the way it is. It presents the opportunity to change anything that emanates from the discussion.

For instance, there may be family treasures or valuable items they might prefer to choose for themselves. It is never safe to assume that X would like Y, and A would like B, when it might be the other way around. Family treasures can be anything from antiques, art, jewellery and coins, to pets, books, musical instruments, electronic equipment and stamp collections. The bequeathing of items of monetary value requested by heirs should be recorded in your Will and supported by bona fide valuation certificates so that the executor may record them accurately in the Liquidation and Distribution account.

Trinkets of no commercial value should be detailed on a typed list indicating who gets what, with every entry signed by the corresponding heir-in-waiting and you. Again, easier to settle before you die and for the executor to carry out.

STEP 2 FOR THE TESTATOR

Get your affairs in order. Sort out your debt. Leaving the executor to catch up on a backlog of personal administration will significantly complicate and slow the process of winding up the estate, much to the frustration of your heirs.

It is of paramount importance that your original signed Will and original codicil (if any) are kept safely. You must inform the nominated executor and a responsible family member of the location of your original Will. If your executor is unable to locate your Will after your demise, it will be nothing short of catastrophic.

It will be necessary to prepare a file containing all original and relevant estate documents, and if original documents are not available, then certified copies of each document so that your executor can attend to the expeditious administration of your estate. The following is a general list of relevant documents that need to be organised, collated, and stored in a file for the assistance of the executor. Some items may not apply to every individual.

If not the original, then certified copies of your:

- Will
- Any signed Codicils
- Living Will if one exists
- National Identity Card/National Identity document and passport
- Medical aid card and statement
- Citizenship papers, if any
- Any Powers of Attorney (which will terminate on death)
- Trust deed/s
- All relevant personal certificates – birth, marriage, divorce, adoption
- Any Ante-Nuptial Agreement
- Title deed/s to properties and mortgage documents

- Car/boat/motorbike/plane registration certificates
- Weapon licences
- Any business documents – employment contracts, partnership agreements, properties, corporation documents and leases
- Any copyrights, patents, and trademarks
- Securities relating to investments: share block certificates and use and occupation agreements, share certificates/portfolio statements and unit trust investment statements
- Insurance policies
- Pension and retirement annuity policies
- Any appraisal certificates for valuables
- Tax number and returns
- Copies of utility accounts and contracts to be transferred or cancelled
- List of banking accounts with account and pin numbers
- List of relatives and friends to contact plus their contact details
- List of advisors with contact details – accountant, attorney, insurance agent.

NOTE: A list of assets is NOT a substitute for a Will.

Ensure that your Will and any codicils are properly signed and witnessed.

STEP 3 FOR THE TESTATOR

Draw up a Declaration of Wishes. Though not legally enforceable, this should clearly set out who you would like to entrust with your more personal items (those of no commercial value) as discussed in Step 1.

The Declaration of Wishes should also detail matters like organ donation and if not recorded in your Will, funeral arrangements, donations to charities and so on.

STEP 4 FOR THE TESTATOR

Choose who you would like to act as your executor, discuss it with the person and solicit agreement. Upon acceptance, discuss your Will with him or her, record the details of all your passwords and access codes and meet regularly to chat about any new developments.

Note: The Master of the High Court will have to approve the nomination of the executor before issuing the Letters of Executorship. The Master may require the executor to furnish a bond of security or be assisted by a specialist, such as an attorney.

TIPS:

If the testator holds significant assets in a Discretionary Living Trust, it will avoid the process, costs and time required to wind them up as part of an estate. Assets that belong to the trust do not form part of the deceased's estate.

Keep a copy of every document in a separate file lest any documents go missing.

MAIN POINTS:

- Ensure that your original Will is kept in a safe place and inform your executor and responsible family member where it is kept.
- Work with the executor and meet regularly to update him/her on any developments.
- Collate all the documents he/she will need to wind up your estate efficiently.

4.
FIRST THINGS FIRST

It is not uncommon for someone to nominate, in their Will, a trusted family member to act as the executor of his estate. Whilst it is not the executor's job to arrange for the death to be reported or for the funeral to be organised, the nominee may choose to help as a kindness to the family. If so, this is what it entails:

REPORTING THE DEATH

The death must be reported and registered at the Department of Home Affairs or South African Police Services (SAPS) station within 5 (five) days from date of death. Not all Home Affairs offices handle the reporting of deaths, so check first or go to SAPS.

Home Affairs and SAPS have the necessary Notice of Death forms. Form DHA-1663A has five sections to be completed. Sections A, B and C must be completed by the authorised medical practitioner/professional nurse responsible for examining the body of the deceased to determine the cause of death. Section D is completed by the person responsible for certifying the identity of the deceased and Section E is completed by the funeral undertaker.

The responsibility for this first administrative task

is often accepted by the undertaker on behalf of the family, providing the undertaker has been appointed and recognised by law. Check with the undertaker first to ensure the reporting process is neither duplicated nor overlooked.

Home Affairs is responsible for issuing the Death Certificate and Death Report once the DHA-1663A form has been processed. If this has been arranged by the undertaker, the certificates are to be delivered to the family. The death certificate must be scrutinised for correction. In many instances the marital status of the deceased is incorrectly set out in the death certificate. The Master will require it to be rectified and this leads to substantial delay in the administration of the estate. It is therefore essential that the correct marital status is included in the death report. The death certificate will be required by the executor to report the estate to the Master's Office. If the death was unnatural, both the death certificate and death report will have to be submitted to the Master's Office.

If the death occurred outside the borders of South Africa, it should be reported to the South African mission, embassy or consulate operating in the country where the death occurred.

The executor will need several originally certified and stamped copies of the Death Certificate, as copies will be required for every instruction given and transaction done on behalf of the estate, like closing accounts, accessing death benefits, and so on.

ARRANGING THE FUNERAL

Meet with the family to discuss the funeral arrangements. Establish who will be paying for the funeral – the family, the estate, or a funeral policy – because the financing will require urgent attention. Most funeral providers require payment upfront.

News of a death usually gets around quite quickly. However, the nominated executor (especially if he/she is a close family member) may be asked to contact a list of key people and advise them of the death and funeral arrangements.

If the type of funeral the deceased wanted has not been prescribed in his Will, the family will decide. The executor will then proceed within these parameters.

A testator should try and take as much guesswork as possible away from the family, as it will reduce their emotional burden significantly.

MAIN POINTS:

- Ensure that the correct marital status is incorporated in the Death Report.
- Scrutinise the death certificate for correctness and, in particular, whether it reflects the correct marital status.
- Attending to these formalities is more of a kindness than an official task for an executor

5.
THE DUTIES OF AN EXECUTOR

Whilst you are required to nominate at least one person in your Will to act as your executor, it is advisable to nominate an alternative person should your first choice become unavailable, or unable to complete the task for whatever reason.

(Note: If an estate is valued at less than R250 000, a Master's representative will be appointed, usually the executor nominated in the Will. He/she is not required to lodge an account of the administration of the estate.)

The duties discussed in this chapter refer to deceased estates with assets valued at R250 000 *or more*.

The Administration of Estates Act, 66 of 1965 governs executorship. The Master of the High Court monitors the process; any attempts to circumvent the system will result in consequences and delays.

The executor's duty is to 1) gather, account for, and secure the estate's assets (both movable, immovable and claims in favour of the estate), 2) pay all debts and taxes due by the estate and, 3) distribute the residue of the estate.

All creditors, expenses and taxes are paid first. Your executor must have the mettle to make tough, difficult decisions in the course of duty, such as, sell cherished property to cover outstanding debt, and have the financial nous to take the necessary proactive measures to protect the residual value of your estate. He/she may only dispose of what is necessary to settle outstanding debt.

In the absence of a contrary provision in the Will, the executor must obtain written consent regarding the manner and conditions of sale from the heirs who have an interest in the asset he/she intends to sell. The sale has also to be approved by the Master, and Capital Gains Tax implications considered. Consent is not required for quoted securities and property realised as a normal business transaction by the executor.

Since he/she is expected to take charge and provide support to your grieving family, meeting them before your demise could provide valuable insights that may help the executor to proceed more constructively when the time comes – for instance, knowing when to solicit their input on important decisions and provide regular updates to them on progress.

If the executor does not already have copies of all the documents required to report your death to the Master, your family may be of assistance. His/her main concern will be to locate and lodge *every* reporting document required at the same time and without delay.

No executor has authority to commence duties until the Master has issued Letters of Executorship in his/her favour, authorising the liquidation and distribution of the estate.

The executor has 14 (fourteen) days to marshal all the information required to report your estate. Ultimately, he/she will have to account to the Master for what you owned (assets) and owed (liabilities) *as at your date of death*. Unnecessary delays caused by the tracking down of elusive documents may impact your heirs materially.

When you die, your estate must be reported in the jurisdiction where you were ordinarily resident prior to your date of death, that is, the area of jurisdiction of a regional division of the High Court, with the Master appointed in respect of that area.

From time of death, your estate will be frozen, and no one may withdraw funds from your bank accounts. If you are married in Community of Property, the joint estate will be frozen – often to the detriment of your surviving spouse and family. Neither may any individual with signing powers on an account of yours withdraw funds from the account – it is classified as fraud. However, with the Master's consent and before the account has lain open for inspection, the executor is authorised to release an amount of money out of the estate which, in his/her opinion, is sufficient to provide for the upkeep of your family or household while the winding up process is underway.

It is also incumbent on the executor to advise your bank that you have passed away. After he/she has received his Letters of Executorship, he/she is required to open a new Estate Late Account in the name of the deceased estate.

One of the preliminary reporting documents (J243) includes a preliminary inventory of assets. It need not be absolutely accurate as 14 days is a relatively short space of time to prepare it. As my introduction suggests, this may already have been prepared and discussed ahead of time with the executor, who may find it helpful to take photographs of rooms to help keep track of the assets, especially if they are valuable. They must not be allowed to disappear during the process and must be properly secured.

The preliminary inventory provides for a listing of immovable property, movable property and claims in favour of the estate. Movable property includes household furniture, unit trusts, shares, etcetera. Claims in favour of the estate include amounts due from current, savings money market accounts from financial institutions, etcetera.

Next, he/she should arrange to protect the estate's assets until they are handed over to the designated beneficiaries. This means properly securing assets like property (including unoccupied property), furniture, cars and so on, to prevent damage, devaluation, or theft. Where possible, he/she should put significant assets to work, earning interest while the process is underway.

Later, he/she may submit a supplementary inventory (J243) of your assets – that is, if other assets have come to light since the initial submission. From there, he/she will collate the assets, pay all outstanding debts and bills as well as the taxes due by the estate, *before* distributing what is left of the estate (the residue) to the heirs named in your Will.

It is a process that also involves the co-operation of

external entities that do not always function as efficiently as they might. He/she may have to keep following up.

How smoothly this process unfolds depends on the administrative preparation carried out by you prior to your death, as well as the complexity of your estate.

IS A NOMINATED EXECUTOR OBLIGED TO ACCEPT THE APPOINTMENT?

No, the nominee has the right to decline – preferably before you die! The main reasons for declining usually include personal issues related to time and experience, geographic location, poor health, or a fear that some form of litigation may be pending, a situation that will not only complicate the process but may put the executor at risk of being named as a defendant.

Executors should be able to take on a meticulously prepared file that includes all the essential reporting documents required to wind up your estate, and a Will that clearly sets out your final wishes. The alternative represents a chaotic paper trail with no quick solution. It will take time and careful sorting to restore order. The heirs are sure to suffer extreme frustration and put pressure on him because they will be expecting access to their inheritance sooner.

If the executor accepts the nomination and is not a specialist, he/she should recruit a specialist as an agent to undertake the administration, because mistakes can prove costly to the estate, and to the executor him/herself.

CAN AN EXECUTOR EXPECT TO BE PAID?

Yes, unless another arrangement has been agreed and recorded in your Will. The recommended executor's fee, as stated in Chapter 2, is 3.5% of the gross value of the assets in the estate and 6% on the gross income.

Travelling costs and other costs such as stationery, postage and telephone charges are not charged separately as they are included in the executor's remuneration. Where the executor incurs exceptional costs, he/she should approach the Master to allow such costs as additional executor's remuneration. Where the executor appoints a specialist agent to administer the estate, the executor must agree the fee with the agent prior to his formal appointment in order to avoid unnecessary disputes.

WHO IS DISQUALIFIED FROM EXECUTORSHIP?

- A person under the age of 18 does not have full legal capacity. However, when this person turns 18, he/she or she may be entitled to appointment as a co-executor.
- Insane people and prodigals (people who, through poor personal conduct, are incapable of managing their own affairs).
- Without proper security, an unrehabilitated insolvent is likely to be disqualified by the Master.
- Partnerships, unless the Letters of Executorship are issued in the names of all the persons who were partners at the time of the testator's passing.

- A person (and his or her spouse) who, on instruction of the testator, signed the Will as a witness, or on behalf of the testator, or who wrote the Will in his or her own handwriting.

MAIN POINTS:

- Winding up an estate is a multi-dimensional assignment, much to learn and much to do – one step at a time.
- The testator's family should work with him/her and be supportive, assisting where they can.

6.
REPORTING AN ESTATE

A) ESTATES WITH ASSETS VALUED AT MORE THAN R250 000

Any deceased person ordinarily resident in the Republic of South Africa at the time of his/her death leaving an estate with assets must have his/her estate wound up according to the Administration of Estates Act, 66 of 1965.

The basic procedure of winding up an estate is set out hereunder:

1. The death must be reported to the Master appointed in the area where the deceased was ordinarily resident within the jurisdiction of the High Court, together with all the supporting documents. The same Master's office will supervise the process.

2. The Master will check the various documents submitted to him. The Acceptance of Trust form, which is also one of the supporting documents, must also be completed, signed, and submitted in duplicate (one copy goes to SARS). If there is more than one appointment of executor, each will be required to submit a separate Acceptance of Trust form. If the

original Will is submitted, the Master will check whether it complies with the requirements of the Will Act, 7 of 1953, and if it does comply, the Master will then register and accept the Will. If the deceased did not leave a Will, then the deceased will have died intestate and one of the supporting documents to be submitted to the Master would be a next-of-kin affidavit to establish who are the next-of-kin of the deceased. If the supporting documents are in order, the Master will issue the Letters of Executorship.

3. On receipt of the Letters of Executorship, the executor will take control of your assets and liabilities. He/she must trace and collate all the necessary information relating to your personal financial affairs – what you owned at your time of death (all movable, immovable assets and claims in favour of the estate) and the administration expenses and other liabilities which need to be paid from the estate.

4. Once all the details have been gathered, he/she will prepare a Liquidation and Distribution account for examination by the Master. The Liquidation and Distribution account will, inter alia, reflect how your estate will be divided and distributed between creditors and heirs.

5. Once the Master has approved the account, it will be advertised (by the executor) to lie for inspection at the Master's office and the magistrate's court (if the deceased was not ordinarily resident within the jurisdiction of the Master's office) for a period of three weeks for public scrutiny. Once the account has

lain for inspection free from objections, the executor must pay all creditors, distribute the residue in accordance with your Will, and lodge proof of distribution to the Master.

6. When all the Master's requirements have been complied with, the Master will issue a formal release that the estate has been filed of record.

All the reporting documents should be submitted together with a covering letter to the Master that stipulates the name of the deceased, and lists the documents submitted.

If the nominee for executorship is not a specialist and no specialist is going to be appointed to assist him/her, the Master may require a bond of security for the full value of the estate, even if the Will specifically exempts the nominated executor from furnishing security. Remember, although exemptions apply to a spouse, parent, or child of the deceased, the Master will insist on a bond of security unless such person is assisted by a specialist.

WHAT DOES THE MASTER DO WHEN HE RECEIVES THE REPORTING DOCUMENTS?

1. He opens a file in the name of the deceased.
2. The documentation is perused by an estate controller for correctness.
3. The Will, if any, is considered by the Master or a Deputy Master or an Assistant Master and is either accepted or rejected.

It has been my experience that very few deceased estates run according to plan, which is why working with a specialist is highly recommended. They have the knowledge and the contacts necessary to help the executor make informed decisions that support progress.

Note: if the deceased had been receiving payments from a pension fund (private, corporate or government), it is important that the nominee executor or family member submitting the documents to the Master, also notifies the pension provider immediately.

When the executor meets with your family a day or two after the funeral, they may be able to assist with any outstanding reporting documents. Since the efficient handling of your estate is in their best interests, they usually like to get the process underway promptly. They could also prove useful regarding the preparation of the personal information the executor will require for the distribution account later – such as addresses, marital status, and sources of income of the beneficiaries.

Reporting documents (plus copies for the executor's own file).

- Originally certified copy of the National Identity Card/Identity Document of the deceased.
- An originally certified copy of the death certificate.
- Death notice (J294).
- Affidavit/declaration re marriage.
- Originally certified copy of the surviving spouse's National Identity Card/Identity Document, if married.
- Originally certified copy of the marriage certificate,

if applicable.
- Preliminary inventory (J243).
- Original Will and any signed codicil.
- Next-of-kin affidavit (if the deceased died intestate or if the beneficiaries are not named in the Will).
- Originally certified copy of the divorce order, if any.
- Nominations for the executor, if the deceased died without a Will.
- Originally certified copy of the nominee executor's National Identity Card/Identity Document.
- Acceptance of Trust (J190), in duplicate, by the nominated executor.

The official documents are available at the Master's website (https://justice.gov.za).

The sooner these documents are submitted, the sooner the Letters of Executorship can be issued. The file will remain with the Master until completion of the process – that is, the Liquidation and Distribution account has been lodged, examined, and approved by a separate division within his offices. The estate is only officially wound up when the Master is satisfied that all the necessary requirements have been met and there is no evidence of fraud.

The fee payable to the Master should be reflected in the Liquidation and Distribution account. Revised in January 2018, it is applied to estates valued over R250 000 and is as follows:

1. There is no Master's fee on estates up to a value of R250 000.

2. On estates valued from R250 000 → R400 000, the fee is R600.

3. On estates valued from R400 000 upwards, the fee is levied at R200 for every R100 000 (up to a maximum fee of R7 500).

You, as testator/testatrix, are advised to keep your Will handy during your lifetime. Check it from time to time. You may discover potential problems regarding validity or interpretation. Rectify it while you have time, with the help of a specialist. If you decide to tinker with it without specialist help, you may very well render it invalid yourself. Effect any changes, usually relating to the birth or death of a beneficiary, sometimes a divorce settlement or to disinherit an individual, and/or if you have sold one or more assets identified in your Will that were destined to be inherited.

B) ESTATES WITH ASSETS VALUED AT R250 000 OR LESS

A deceased estate valued at a value of R250 000 or less is simpler to wind up.

The Master of the High Court may dispense with the Letters of Executorship and issue Letters of Authority in terms of Section 18(3) of the Administration of Estates Act 66 of 1965. This entitles the nominated representative to administer the estate without following the full procedure set out in the Act.

The process of winding up an estate that is R250 000 *or less*:

1. Your nominated executor must report your estate and submit all the necessary documents at the relevant regional office of the Master of the High Court. Its administration will be supervised by the same office.

2. An Acceptance of Trust form will not be required. Instead, the nominated executor should complete and submit the Acceptance of Master's Directions form (J155).

3. Once the Master is satisfied that all the documents meet the necessary requirements, he will issue the Letters of Authority (J170) in terms of which the representative is duly authorised to take control of the assets of the deceased estate, to pay the debts and to transfer the residue of the estate to the heir/s entitled thereto by law.

4. The advertising requirements are dispensed with. No Master's fees are payable and there is no need to open an estate banking account or to submit a Liquidation and Distribution account to the Master for approval. All the supporting documents which need to be submitted to the Master for an estate with assets valued at more than R250 000,00 are also required to be submitted. However, an Acceptance of Trust is not required as no executor is being appointed. The Master will require a list of creditors. The value ascribed to the assets in the inventory will have to be duly vouched and these vouchers will have to be submitted to the Master. The difficulty is that the banks will not furnish the information to

the nominated representative. The representative will therefore have to visit the Master's office and obtain a Letter of Authorisation addressed to the bank instructing them to furnish the information to the nominated representative so that the assets are correctly reflected in the inventory and in the Letters of Authority.

For more information on the winding up of deceased estates and the Administration of Estates Act 66 of 1965, go to https://justice.gov.za.

NOTE: The R250 000 value mentioned is reviewed by the Minister of Justice from time to time. The process may be simpler but adherence to the administrative protocols is inescapable.

7.
REPORTING DOCUMENTS EXPLAINED

THE NOTIFICATION PROCESS

The Administration of Estates Act, 66 of 1965 was promulgated to consolidate and amend the law relating to the Liquidation and Distribution of the estates of deceased persons, the administration of property of minors and persons under curatorship, to regulate the rights of beneficiaries and to provide for matters incidental thereto.

There is no legal requirement for a formal reading of your Will, but the nominated executor should, as a courtesy to your beneficiaries, advise them in writing that they have been named in it.

A pre-prepared list of external people (with contact details) who have been assisting you with your personal and financial affairs in recent years would also be very useful.

The following explanations provide some clarity on the essential reporting documents.

DEATH NOTICE (J294)

A simple, self-explanatory one-page document that will require your personal details. The person reporting your death can either access and complete it online, or download it from the Master's website (www.justice.gov.za/master/deceased-how.html).

For ease of administration, it is preferable to have the Death Notice signed by the surviving spouse or partner of the deceased, and if there is no surviving spouse or partner, a close blood relative or a person closely connected to the deceased residing in the district in which the death has taken place. It records, inter alia, the name of the deceased, his/her identity number, marital status and information regarding the spouse and children, both surviving and predeceased and, if predeceased, the lawful issue (that is, children born to parents, regardless of their parents' marital status) of such pre-deceased child. It also records the name of any pre-deceased or divorced spouse and, if predeceased, the date of death and estate reference number.

If married at time of death, and the marriage took place and is governed by the laws of a country other than the Republic of South Africa, Zimbabwe or the United Kingdom, additional documents will be necessary to determine the proprietary consequences of the marriage. These documents are usually obtained from the consulate or a legal practitioner of that country.

The form also needs to record the ordinary place(s) of residence of the deceased during the 12 months prior to death.

If it transpires that some of the necessary information was entered incorrectly or omitted when the Death Notice was originally lodged, an amended death notice may be lodged at a later stage.

DEATH CERTIFICATE

The original or an originally certified copy of the death certificate must be lodged with the Master to prove the death of the deceased. It is immaterial whether the signatory was present at the death of the deceased or identified the deceased after his/her death. It is essential to check the death certificate for correctness.

If you die of natural causes, the undertakers usually make the necessary arrangements to obtain the Death Certificate from the Department of Home Affairs. Several certified copies will be required to wrap up many aspects of your estate.

If you die of unnatural causes, the death certificate will reflect that the cause of death was unnatural or under investigation. In such a case a post mortem examination is usually done and sometimes an inquest is held.

PRELIMINARY INVENTORY (J243)

This template is available on the Master's website.

The preliminary inventory will help determine the category in which your estate belongs (R250 000 or less, or more than R250 000). If all indications are that your estate will not exceed R250 000 in value, it may be reported to the Master or the nearest Magistrates' offices, which are designated service points for the regional Master's offices. (Estate figures quoted are relevant to 2023.)

With respect to joint estates, the inventory must reflect all the assets of the joint estate. For couples married in Community of Property, the assets of both spouses (and who owns them) must be included.

The values of the various items may not be readily ascertainable without valuation certificates but as a preliminary inventory, the executor is allowed a little latitude. Items listed as "value to be ascertained" are acceptable until bona fide valuation certificates can be obtained. Errors discovered in the original inventory can also be corrected by lodging an amended version at a later stage.

Immovable property should be dealt with first, thereafter movable property, and thereafter claims in favour of the estate.

IMMOVABLE PROPERTY

All immovable properties must be listed in the preliminary inventory. These also include sectional title units and any exclusive use areas held by notarial deed of cession of exclusive use areas. The immovable properties must be described in accordance with the title deed descriptions. The title deed number under which the property is held must be disclosed. The value ascribed to each property is usually the municipal valuation. The valuation is obtained from the rates utility bill issued by the municipality. Municipal valuations can also sometimes be assessed on municipal websites. It is also prudent to obtain deed searches for each property in order to confirm the property description and ownership details.

Farm properties may be more difficult to sort out as they fall under the Subdivision of Agricultural Land Act 70 of 1970 and may also be affected by current land reform initiatives.

MOVABLE PROPERTY

The executor should compile the inventory with your family present to eliminate disputes at a later stage.

- Clothes are generally regarded as having no saleable value, unless they include items such as high-end branded accessories, fur coats, etcetera.
- General household furniture may also have no saleable value but items that have been bequeathed should be listed.
- Jewellery.
- Unit trust investments.
- All quoted and unquoted shares.
- Shares in private companies.
- Interests in business partnerships. If the loan account is in credit, it must reflect in the inventory. Similarly, these particulars should also identify your share of the partnership liabilities for use later in the Liquidation and Distribution account.
- Motor vehicle/s – make, year of manufacture and registration number.
- Any other valuable modes of transport like specialised bicycles, boats, yachts, and planes.

- Livestock.
- Farm equipment.
- Firearms – Ensure that your executor has a list of every firearm you own, together with their corresponding licenses and the information detailing where they are stored. They must be recorded in the inventory, preferably with the manufacturer's number. The executor will then take responsibility for the safekeeping of the firearm/s and ammunition, preferably with a licensed gunsmith or dealer.

Once the Letters of Executorship have been issued, the Commissioner of the South African Police Services must receive a copy of the list of firearms, plus their details (make, calibre and serial number) quantity of firearms and ammunition, your name and last address as the deceased owner and the address where the firearm/s and ammunition are being held. A copy of the Death Notice and the names, addresses and identity documents/cards of each beneficiary must be included. Every three months, the executor is required to report in writing to the Commissioner with information regarding the progress made and the measures being taken to dispose of the firearm/s and ammunition.

It is advisable to have the inventory signed by a responsible person (such as a surviving spouse or partner) and to keep copies of all the documents submitted.

Making provision for pets that may outlive you is covered in chapter 17.

CLAIMS IN FAVOUR OF THE ESTATE (for the attention of the executor)

Claims in favour of the estate, as the name suggests, are claims that are payable to the estate. The following are examples of claims payable to the estate:

- Amount due from a deposit taking institution under a current/savings/ and fixed deposit investment account. The executor is also advised to record the corresponding bank branches.
- Amount due under an insurance policy payable to the estate.
- Any amount due in respect of undrawn salary, leave pay or bonuses.
- Amount due under a loan account.
- Any amount due from SARS.

ACCEPTANCE OF TRUST (J190)

This must be completed in duplicate by the nominated executor and lodged at the Master's office, together with the first (reporting) set of documents required after your passing. A certified copy of his National Identity Card/ Identity Document must accompany the Acceptance of Trust form.

The Master will transmit the duplicate copy of the Acceptance of Trust form to the South African Revenue Services so that they can determine whether they have a claim for outstanding income tax against the estate or any refunds are owed to the estate.

Any co-executors nominated must submit separate

Acceptance of Trust forms together with copies of their National Identity Cards/ Identity Documents.

If your Will nominates an unspecified partner of a law or accounting firm as executor, the partners of the firm are required to send a letter signed by them to the Master. In it, they nominate the specific partner who will undertake the executor's role and he or she signs the Letters of Acceptance.

BOND OF SECURITY

The bond is obtainable from an insurance company. Its purpose is to cover the estate, as well as any minors or person under curatorship, for any losses incurred by the executor. It holds him or her personally liable for any failure to perform the function properly or for any form of maladministration that results in losses to the estate.

In order to be granted a Bond of Security, the executor must submit a proposal form (available at the insurance company) and the Bond of Security form (available on the Master's website and at his offices). It must be lodged in duplicate.

The rates for premiums are levied as a percentage of the gross assets of the estate, payable annually until the estate has been finalised.

As is sometimes the case, if further assets come to light after the documents have been lodged with the Master, a supplementary inventory will be required. The insurance company must be notified so they can adjust the value of the bond and the corresponding premium, and issue an endorsement. The endorsement and supplementary inventory should then be relodged with the Master.

PREPARATION

The Letters of Executorship may take a few weeks to be issued, which means that the nominated executor cannot commence any official processes that require him/her to present Letters of Executorship. Once the Letters have been issued, the executor is now authorised to liquidate and distribute the deceased estate. He/she is now entitled to take possession of all the estate property and documents until all creditors and beneficiaries have been paid and the estate duly finalised.

During this time, the executor may want to get started with preparing files and the inventory. If there is any suspicion that property is being concealed or withheld for whatever reason, he/she may apply to a magistrate for a search warrant.

Whether collated as hard copies or electronically, it is suggested that the executor commences file preparation. The following is a guide to the various files that need to be prepared:

- Will
- Appraisals
- Bank account (Estate)
- Bank accounts (Personal)
- Bills (paid)
- Bills (unpaid)

- Certificates (birth, marriage, ante-nuptial agreements, divorce)
- Employment contracts
- Funeral (burial/cremation)
- Life insurance and annuities
- Income tax (personal)
- Income tax
- Trust documents
- Medical expenses
- Pensions
- Property inventory
- Real estate contracts
- Retirement accounts
- Stocks and bonds
- Child support documents
- Business co-ownership agreements
- Medical aid correspondence
- Registration papers for vehicles, boats etc
- Master
- Correspondence with beneficiaries
- Rental agreement & termination advice
- Memberships with professional organisations, clubs, or gyms. Memberships may need to be cancelled, and fee refunds investigated. The executor will also need the details of your social media accounts, email addresses and the charities that have been receiving regular support from you. If not clarified in your Will, continuation or cancellation will have to be decided.

With most of the preparation already under his belt,

your executor will have the crucial advantage of being able to hit the road running and complete the process faster than most. Your family stands to reap the benefits of a smoother winding-up process and quicker access to their material legacy.

MAIN POINTS:

- Comprehensive administrative preparation by the testator will support the executor and help facilitate the process of winding up an estate, to the advantage of the heirs.
- A primed executor can proceed with greater efficiency.
- Executorship is multi-faceted and administratively time-consuming.

8.
PREPARE THE EXECUTOR TO GET THE BALL ROLLING

The Letters of Executorship usually take a few weeks to be processed and approved.

Meanwhile, the nominated executor can proceed with obtaining originally certified copies of his/her National Identity Card/Identity Document and proof of his/her residential address as well as the death certificate, as these documents will be required for submission to deposit taking institutions and other entities like SARS.

If you live alone and the property you own will be unoccupied when you pass, the executor must ensure that the property is appropriately secured and that the electricity and water supplies are turned off. He/she should know, or check, whether the property is insured for fire and theft. If a beneficiary is prejudiced or suffers financial loss arising from a failure of the executor to insure property, the executor may be held liable for such loss. Discuss this with him/her while you can. If there are any valuable items at your property, he/she should remove them for safekeeping and notify the beneficiaries of the action taken. Naturally, he/she must notify the insurers of your passing and provide them with a copy of his Letters of Executorship once they are issued.

Your Will is a key component and not a private matter. Here are three points to ponder:

- It is mandatory to lodge the Will of a deceased person at the appropriate Master's office.
- Every Will lodged is open to public scrutiny.
- Since the information contained in a Will is not private, individuals with a specific personal interest in it may want to investigate the contents, which could then lead to legal challenges before the ink has even dried on the executor's Letters of Executorship.

Here is something else to ponder: If you want to protect your assets and private business from prying eyes after you die, consider setting up a Discretionary Living Trust during your lifetime. Once your assets are transferred into the Trust, ownership (but not enjoyment) of Trust assets shifts to the Trustees. Any aggrieved party who feels entitled to some of the spoils in your estate would be thwarted, for how can they access what you do not own?

Also, information pertaining to your Trust remains confidential and inaccessible to unnamed parties and, since the distribution of assets will flow from the Trust (not the Will), estate duty will not apply to Trust assets.

Your executor should bear in mind that your beneficiaries will not only be able to obtain a copy of your Will, but all the other documents submitted to the Master – including the Liquidation and Distribution account.

The executor will be required to prepare or obtain supporting vouchers for all assets and liabilities disclosed in the Liquidation and Distribution account. Where the deceased dies intestate, the share of the minors will be paid into the Guardian's Fund. Where the deceased died leaving a Will, the inheritance awarded to a minor child will be paid over in accordance with the provisions of the Will. It will be paid to the trustees if a testamentary trust has been created, or to the legal guardian if that is what the Will provides. If the Will makes no provision in this regard, payment will be made into the Guardian's Fund.

1. *Assets and liabilities*

    The Master will require professional appraisals of all movable and immovable property that is declared on the preliminary inventory, plus any other property that may since have come to light. Values should be calculated at date of death.

    Institutions that can assist with this information can be notified and asked to prepare the requisite documents. They will require originally certified copies of the Letters of Executorship, the National Identity Card/Identity Document of the executor and proof of his/her residential address, as well as the death certificate before they can release the information to the executor.

    It would help if you were to provide the executor with mortgagee statements/loan account information ahead of time.

    In the case of *foreign assets,* the executor will

com-municate with the institutions concerned to obtain the particulars of the assets and establish what is required to proceed. He/she will have to work with specialists who live in the country where the assets are held. They will require an official copy of the death certificate and court-certified copies of the Letters of Executorship. It is imperative that he/she advises the Master when applying for the copies that they are to be used in a foreign country as these copies will have to be duly authenticated by the Master under his seal and signature for use outside the Republic. A cost for the copies will be incurred.

Do you have any timeshares? The managing agents will be able to provide the executor with a valuation based on unit sales history and advise on how ownership may be transferred to a beneficiary or sold.

2. Get to grips with the *accounts* so the executor will know what is due on:
   - Utility accounts – municipal, water, electricity, and gas.
   - Other accounts – levy statements, mobile phone contracts, TV subscriptions, internet service providers, store cards, gym, and club memberships.
   - Debts owed to individuals.
   - Outstanding taxes.

A key administrative responsibility and legal requirement for the executor is to determine the full extent of your liabilities. This requires him/her to publish a notice in the *Government Gazette* and at least one local newspaper circulated in the area in which you ordinarily lived, calling for creditors to come forward and lodge their claims against your estate. Creditors have 30 days from date of publication to respond to the notice.

3. Get to grips with your *debit orders* so the executor knows who must be notified and which should be cancelled:
    - Bank accounts – current, savings, fixed term, mortgages, overdrafts, credit cards, loans.
    - Medical aid contributions.
    - Insurance policy contributions.
    - Car repayments.

4. Prepare the *Power of Attorney* for signature.
    - If the executor is going to handle the entire administrative process, then no Power of Attorney is required. He/she will need to approach the bank and other institutions to ascertain their requirements for obtaining certificates of balances and payment of the proceeds.
    - If he/she decides to appoint an independent agent to handle the process, then a Power of Attorney nominating the agent will have to be prepared, signed by the executor, and duly witnessed. Note: The Power of Attorney does not transfer liability to the Agent. The executor

remains liable while the estate is being wound up by the Agent.

5. Check your *ante-nuptial contract*, if applicable.
   - If this was not discussed with the executor, he/she will have to establish if the accrual system applies.
   - Also, it is not uncommon for one spouse to make a donation to the other. For example, in an ante-nuptial contract, a husband may cede a policy on his life to his wife. If you have ceded a life policy to your spouse (or any third party) check the consequences if he or she predeceases you. Who gets the money?

     Verify whether your life policy includes a *reversionary condition.* It simplifies the situation because it stipulates, on the happening of a specific event (like death), ownership of the policy should revert to the donor (you). *Then nominate an alternative beneficiary without delay.* In the absence of a reversionary condition, the executor will need the services of a specialist.

6. *If you were divorced,* the executor will require a copy of the *order of divorce and settlement agreement* to check for contractual obligations to your former spouse.
   - Any maintenance claims due to your former spouse – provisions in the agreement of divorce must be fulfilled unless the divorce agreement

has an alternative proviso. The terms of the divorce agreement will determine how he/she should proceed.

- If, however, no such provision was made in the divorce agreement and the surviving spouse was granted a maintenance order in terms of section 7 (2) of the Divorce Act 70 of 1979, the order will fall away when the maintaining party dies.

A former spouse might want to institute a claim against the estate. The executor may enter into an agreement with your former spouse to pay a lump sum. The usual method of computation is to calculate the present value of future expenses by discounting the projected expenses, allowing for inflation, interest and the dependent's probability of survival.

Both parents owe a duty of support to a child, even after death. If, however, you die and have made no provision in your Will for the ongoing maintenance of a child (and the dependent child has no or insufficient means of his or her own), the child will have a claim for maintenance against the estate. This is also calculated according to a table in the Estate Duty Act that assesses the present value of the amount required for the anticipated period of dependency.

The executor should note that creditors' claims trump maintenance claims.

7. *Income tax*

    Since SARS will require a copy of the final Liquidation and Distribution account, transparency is crucial. If SARS has any concerns about the final account, it can lodge an objection. This will not only slow the winding up process and frustrate the beneficiaries, but it will compound the executor's workload. If your estate is substantial and complicated, he/she should find a specialist and:

    - Obtain a copy of your last tax return to SARS.
    - Send a certified copy of your death certificate as well as copies of your Will and preliminary inventory to SARS.
    - At the same time, request that SARS sends any outstanding tax returns for completion.
    - If you were not registered as a taxpayer, the executor is advised to check your tax and income history to determine why you were not registered, and then forward all the information to SARS. This would include interest payments from any investments registered in your name, going back five or more years. Accruals on investments are of particular interest to SARS and the estate's tax returns must reflect these sums as at date of death.

8. *Capital Gains Tax*

    When you die, you are deemed to have disposed of your assets at market value on the date of your death.

    The assets that *devolve to a surviving spouse are*

free of capital gains tax as roll-over provisions apply. However, should those assets be disposed of by the surviving spouse during his/her lifetime, then the base cost would be the value at which the deceased spouse acquired the assets. Similarly, if the assets are not disposed of, then on the death of the surviving spouse the base cost will be the value at which the deceased spouse acquired the assets.

Capital Gains Tax is highly complex, and since death triggers the disposal of assets and the disposal of assets triggers CGT, the executor will have to deal with it. A specialist should be consulted.

9. *Accrual claims*

Your executor will need to establish whether you were married under the accrual system to determine which way the accrual lies, and whether it is an asset or a liability in terms of the estate. An affidavit by your surviving spouse should be drafted and used as a voucher in support of the item.

10. *Quoted companies and mutual funds*

The executor should approach the JSE or your broker or the relevant company for a valuation certificate as at the date of death and obtain information whether any dividends may have accrued but have not yet been paid. These should be recorded as assets in the estate and reflected in the income tax return to date of death. Payment of any dividends due to the estate are likely to be withheld until the Letters of

Executorship have been issued, the estate bank account opened, and FICA has been updated.

11. *Unquoted companies and close corporations*
    The executor must contact the auditor or accounting officer and request a valuation of your shareholding or member's interest as at your date of death – preferably approved by SARS. At the same time, he/she should ask for any certificates relating to debit or credit loan accounts, dividends paid or accrued and director's fees as at your date of death. Once received, if the valuation does not carry SARS approval, he/she should forward the valuations on to SARS together with balance sheets for the previous three years. He/she should also investigate whether there are any shareholders' or members' agreements (or articles or founding statements) that relate the disposal of shares or a member's interest when a shareholder or member dies.

12. *Banks and other financial institutions*
    The executor is duty-bound to contact the specific departments from which he/she needs information. Certificates will be required from each department reflecting the balances of individual accounts (current, savings, credit card, mortgages, loans), plus any interest accrued to each account at date of death. Income tax certificates to the same effect will be expected by SARS. He/she should also diarise maturity dates of any fixed-term investments.

If married in Community of Property, your surviving spouse may ask the executor to send a written request to the bank/s holding any joint current or savings accounts, to ask that such account/s are not frozen and remain fully accessible. Assurance of solvency will be required. If the request is not met, the surviving spouse should be advised to open an account in his or her own name so that any regular revenue stream (such as pension payouts) may continue.

13. *Life insurance policies*

The executor must contact the insurance company you used to determine how any life policies should be handled. As executor he/she will require:

- Estate Duty certificates that reflect the amount/s payable, and to whom (beneficiaries).
- Information regarding any policy that was ceded as security for a debt owed by you. The full amount payable according to the terms of the policy must be reflected as an asset in the Liquidation and Distribution account, and any amount payable recorded as a liability. The proceeds of mortgage protection policies which are paid to the mortgagee are not disclosed in the Liquidation and Distribution account, but any surplus amount should be reflected.

The insurance company will advise on their claim requirements.

14. *Pension*

    You should contact your employer for information regarding any death benefits payable. Any lump sum payments from group life pension funds or retirement annuities may be subject to tax. Whilst the insurance company is responsible for obtaining the tax directive from SARS, an executor should follow up to avoid unanticipated claims later in the process.

15. *Short-term insurance*

    The executor will also have to find out whether you had any short-term insurance policies in your name, such as householder's and car insurance. He/she must first establish whether the policies are still in force, then find out whether they are to be taken over by another party, usually a surviving spouse. If they are to be taken over, the insurance company should be informed, and approached to endorse the policy so that the responsibility and interest for the item is assigned to the new owner. If the items covered are sold or given away, the executor should inform the insurance company and instruct them to cancel the policy and refund the proportionate amount of the last premium paid.

16. *Undrawn salary and leave pay*

    The executor should also approach your employer to ascertain what amounts are due in terms of undrawn salary or leave pay. He/she is then required to record the gross amount as an asset in the Liquidation and Distribution account, and any deductions (such as medical aid, PAYE, or pension contributions) entered as liabilities. Since the Letters of Executorship require a bank account to be opened for the estate, the transfer from the employer to the deceased estate account may be delayed. To avoid any oversights, he/she should diarise to notify the deceased's employer of the account details once they are available.

17. *Mortgage bonds*
   - If you owned a property that is mortgaged, the executor must obtain a certificate that reflects the amount owing as at date of death.
   - If the property was let, the certificate required should reflect the amount of interest, insurance premiums, assessment rates and other expenses paid during the relevant tax periods. You should investigate whether there is loan protection cover for the liability under the mortgage bond.

The executor must also write to the bondholder for the bond and title deeds (or copies thereof), then establish whether your surviving spouse is able to maintain the monthly bond repayments. If not, approach the bondholder and request the suspension of payments until funds become available. Financial institutions are usually amenable to a grace period of around 3 months. You should investigate whether an insurance policy exists that covers such amounts.

18. *Rent*

    The Letters of Executorship are required before the executor can collect any rental on immovable property. Owing to limited contractual capacity, no executor may enter into a lease on behalf of the estate – unless so authorised in your Will, or by court. However, the beneficiary to whom the property will devolve has the legal capacity to enter into a lease.

19. *Liabilities*

    Funeral expenses are an allowable deduction and should be included in the Liquidation and Distribution account. These expenses should be fair and reasonable. Exorbitant expenditure will be disallowed. The actual costs for the coffin, hearse, grave digging, or cremation will be allowed. It has been practice not to allow the cost of a tombstone as a tombstone is strictly not a funeral expense.

    The executor can get the ball rolling on a number of these points but access to the actual documents will only be possible once his/her Letters of Executorship have been issued.

MAIN POINTS:

- Collate as much of the information for the executor ahead of time as is reasonably possible.
- The executor should use the waiting period to become familiar with all the information so he/she can hit the ground running when the Letters are received.

9.
SECURE YOUR SUPPORT TEAM

With executorship comes liability. The right team of reliable and relevant specialists is essential. You may have some suggestions, but ultimately the executor must source his team responsibly and be confident in their ability to deliver the standard of work that is required of them. No "friends of friends" offering to do the work for significantly less! The people he/she is most likely to need:

AN ATTORNEY

Since most people are not accustomed to handling contentious legal, financial and inheritance issues, there are specialists the executor should seriously consider appointing to help wind up your estate. Crucially, they are familiar with the regulations contained in the Administration of Estates Act 66 of 1965 (and other pertinent Acts) and will know how to overcome any legal obstacles. They are also skilled negotiators who know how to manage beneficiary disputes, arrange settlement terms with creditors or handle an ex-spouse wanting to lay claim to a portion of your estate. Dealing in uncharted territory and lacking the necessary experience could cost the estate dearly and precipitate a lawsuit for damages.

If you have not yet approached the important "when I die" talk with your family and used it as an opportunity to straighten out any quarrelsome matters, the time to sort it out is now. You may also discover that your beneficiaries would prefer that the current asset distribution be adjusted to accommodate their future plans.

After your death, a redistribution trade-off amongst themselves could be implemented – for example, full ownership of a property instead of an equal share in an investment portfolio. Any redistribution of bequeathed property must be equal in value. A Redistribution Agreement should be drawn up by this specialist, as the terms will have to be negotiated and the Agreement submitted to the Master with the Liquidation and Distribution account.

This specialist is also a very useful ally if your executor is required to sell fixed property or vacant land that belongs to the estate. External input on the property sale contract and proper process is invaluable.

Executors have an obligation to protect the estate's assets and avoid losses. If an agent is not appointed, he/she is advised to consider legal consultations carefully and limit them to issues beyond his/her capabilities.

AN ACCOUNTANT

What does the average person know about the taxes due on a deceased estate, what and how they are applied or what qualifies as a legitimate deduction? The executor must take care not to contravene any of the taxation laws of the country and should preferably arrange for a specialist to prepare the estate's tax returns. All the relevant tax certificates and other supporting documents will need to be made available to the specialist.

This specialist can also advise on any tax implications associated with actions the executor may be planning to take – like selling certain assets to cover outstanding debts – and assist with the preparation of the final Liquidation and Distribution account required by the Master.

AN APPRAISER

Executors are required to approach accredited and reputable appraisers to have relevant items correctly valued. Items of significance like antiques, jewellery, art, cars, shares, collections (stamps, coins, weapons and so on), will need a specialist appraiser in each field. Thumb-suck valuations are also ill-advised because what appears to be expensive may not be, and vice versa. Diamonds and cubic zirconia are a case in point.

It is about fairness. If a Will stipulates that all assets should be divided among the beneficiaries "in equal shares", the executor must first establish the correct value of each asset before he/she is able to divide the estate equitably. Bona fide valuations help establish a tax basis, meet the executor's fiduciary duty, and provide protection from lawsuits.

The certificates of valuation should reflect the date-of-death value and be filed safely, as the information will be required for the drawing of the Liquidation and Distribution account.

AN ESTATE AGENT

An accredited real estate appraiser will be required to value residential, commercial, or business property. Also, if the Will requires that immovable property should be sold, the executor will need to appoint a reputable estate agent or auctioneer to list, market, negotiate and sell the property. If the property requires attention, the executor should seek advice as the condition of the property will influence the selling price.

A CONTRACTOR

A rundown property earmarked for sale will need a contractor to assess the extent of the repairs to make it saleable. In some cases, the executor may have to decide whether the cost-to-sale price ratio makes it worthwhile.

The contractor to be avoided is someone's retired "handyman" uncle or his assistant's boyfriend, even if they have promised the world to do the job cheaper than anyone else. It is obligatory to find a "tried and trusted" contractor, someone with experience, a proven track record and a reputation to protect, lest any recourse on the quality of workmanship becomes necessary. The executor should ask the contractor for a quotation on the scope of work to be done and the estimated completion time, then discuss this with the specialist who is assisting, as a contract may be necessary to define the scope of work, quality of workmanship and time frames. He/she should never undertake this unadvisedly as any calamities that incur losses to the estate will end up costing him or her money. He/she should monitor the progress regularly and take remedial action where necessary.

AN AUCTIONEER

The executor may also decide to dispose of certain movable property by public auction. An experienced auctioneer will be able to separate the items of value from the sentimental pieces.

AN INSURANCE AGENT

Once the death of a policy holder has been reported to the insurance agent or company by a family member or the executor, life insurance generally solves an immediate liquidity problem for the nominated beneficiary, most commonly the surviving spouse. An insurance agent should advise the beneficiary to spend such funds in a thrifty and circumspect manner until the administration of the estate is completely finalised, especially since there are chronic service delivery issues in many of the Master's offices.

If you nominated a Discretionary Living Trust as the beneficiary of the life policy, control of distributions from the Trust would fall to the Trustees and put paid to any ideas of reckless splurging.

Chances are you will have an individual who has handled your insurance requirements over the years.

After ensuring that any insurance funds due to the family are paid, the executor should check with him to see whether any other policies remain in force and if so, how they should be claimed or cancelled. Thereafter, check that any existing insurances over assets (home, vehicle, business, valuable personal property and so on) are kept up to date. As he/she is accountable for all immovable and movable property, the executor should ensure that all assets of value are comprehensively insured against loss or damage.

A BANKER

The executor is required to open a transactional account in the name of the estate. All existing bank accounts should be closed, and the banks instructed to pay the proceeds into the estate late bank account. The executor may place any surplus funds in the transactional account into an estate late investment/call account with any recognised financial institution. Debit orders on any of the existing accounts will have to be cancelled.

Debt owed by you does not die with you. It must be settled by the estate before any distributions can be made to beneficiaries. Therefore, it is suggested that the executor discusses the implications of your debt with the banker (mortgages, credit cards, loans, overdrafts and so on) and come to an arrangement. If there are insufficient funds in the estate to cover the total debt, assets may have to be sold to raise the necessary capital.

A BROKER

While the estate winding up process is underway, the executor may identify some unproductive assets in need of attention. A good broker should have some recommended options to discuss with him/her.

The executor may discover that you had securities (stocks and bonds) as part of your financial portfolio. Stocks are shares of ownership in a corporation and depending on how well the corporation is performing, a portion of the corporate profits may be paid as dividends to stockholders.

Bonds are debt investments (or loans) to a corporation or government that pays interest on its loans, a portion of which goes to the bondholder. A collective investment scheme is run by a fund manager, who pools the money from many investors to purchase securities.

Securities produce three kinds of taxable income: interest, dividends, and capital gains (or losses). The executor is required to monitor the value of the estate and take corrective measures to improve investment performance and reduce taxes where necessary.

There are also financial mechanisms that provide for retirement – like annuities. The point is, if the executor is not particularly acquainted with complex financial matters and needs guidance, he/she should discuss this with the broker. Liquidating productive stock to raise capital should be avoided if there is cash available. Electronic access to account information will help him/her monitor the investments and make more informed decisions.

Remember, the buck stops with the executor (not the broker) and distribution through liquidation carries costs and tax implications.

MAIN POINTS:

- The Executor will need a reliable support team and you may have a list of trustworthy contacts. Any poor advice or shoddy management will cost him/her dearly.
- Have the "when I die" conversation and address any issues while you can.

10.
THE SORTING AND DISPOSAL OF ASSETS

While the executor is in the process of sorting out a support team, he/she should check your Will to determine who is to receive which assets, and when those assets should be distributed, as you may have included an age determination.

If you discussed the disposal of assets with your beneficiaries ahead of time, each person knows what to expect. However, no asset may be distributed until all outstanding estate debt has been paid, the Master of the High Court has received all the necessary documents and accepted the Liquidation and Distribution account, and such account has lain for inspection free from objections. This is to ensure that there are no objections to the account in case some or all may have to be sold to settle estate debt.

The executor then needs to establish who would like which of the items not specifically bequeathed and which have no commercial value.

ASSETS OF NO COMMERCIAL VALUE

The assets the executor should sort include:

- personal property – a very general term that covers anything from books, pictures, and computers,
- personal effects – have a more intimate connation that refers to items that someone would wear or carry,
- household items – a very general term that covers anything from curtains to cutlery.

These items not bequeathed in your Will hold sentimental or practical significance rather than material value. Residuary heirs are entitled to claim such items, so the executor should keep a record of who wants what, place them in a box labelled "Bequests" and store them in a safe place. If there is rivalry over a particular item, the executor will have to act as referee and secure an agreement between the rivals.

It is worth noting that a list of items designated for specific individuals recorded by you during your lifetime (but excluded from the Will), is not legally binding. Neither are verbal claims that you promised a particular item to someone. If said item is not in your Will, the executor is under no obligation to acquiesce to the request.

AUCTION PILE

The next pile to focus on relates to the items that might be auctioned, those items not claimed at the "Bequests" meeting. Since the executor is unlikely to know what is saleable, the items identified for auction should be tagged, recorded and transported to the auctioneer.

Auctioneers work on a commission basis, usually a percentage on the items sold. Keep proof of sale and proof that the proceeds of such sale have been paid into the bank account.

JUNK PILE

The last pile represents the waste disposer's lot. Need exceeds supply in South Africa and acts of charity are generally well received. The executor is advised to discuss his/her intentions with your family ahead of time lest they have any special requests regarding their disposal, perhaps to a specific charity. Naturally, the collection should be supervised by him/her. Family members may choose to be present, or not, but it is advisable that the executor has one independent witness to support that the disposal was undertaken correctly.

MAIN POINTS:

- Be precise about material bequests in your Will.
- The executor should consult with the residuary heirs with regard to the disposal of any assets not specifically bequeathed in your Will.

11.
HOW TO OBTAIN VALUATIONS ON MOVABLE AND IMMOVABLE PROPERTY

The executor may be tasked with obtaining credible appraisements on the movable and immovable property that forms part of your estate, usually where there are minor children or estate duty implications.

He/she may require appraisements to establish the net value of your estate as this will determine your estate's dutiable value after an abatement of R3.5 million has been applied.

The Master may also request an appraisement under certain circumstances, generally based on –

- whether the executor was required to furnish security,
- your Will or beneficiaries specifically request property valuations,
- a trustee is to receive a benefit from your Will,
- a section 38 taking over is to be instituted by a surviving spouse (The Administration of Estates Act of 1965.) Available exclusively to a surviving spouse,

a section 38 taking over is sometimes instituted to preserve the family home for the protection of minor children.

Section 38 provides that the Master may authorise the making over of property to the surviving spouse under four specific conditions: 1) one of two spouses, whether married in or out of community of property, has died, 2) the deceased has made no provision to the contrary in any Will or other testamentary provision, 3) the major heirs and any claimants against the estate consent, and 4) it appears to him that no person interested would be prejudiced thereby. Then, subject to security being given for the payment of any minor's share, and subject to such other conditions as the Master may determine, to make over to the surviving spouse any, all, in whole or in part of that portion of the deceased's property, at a valuation to be made by an appraiser, or any other person approved by the Master.

If the executor is uncertain about the valuations he/she is required to furnish, the Master may be contacted for clarity. In a typical estate, the Master is likely to accept that personal apparel and effects have no saleable value and may be reflected as such on the preliminary inventory. If, however, any items have been specially bequeathed in your Will, they should carry an individual value and be itemised in the Liquidation and Distribution account.

Appraisers for the valuation of property are appointed by the Minister, or an officer of the Department of Justice delegated thereto in writing by the Minister in terms of Section 6 of the Administration of Estates Act. This function has been delegated to the Office of the Chief Master. The Chief Master has compiled a list of appraisers in different areas of the country, but unfortunately the list is outdated and needs to be updated.

1. MOVABLE PROPERTY

Any items of significant value and deemed to be dutiable should be appraised by an expert. The most obvious valuables are cars, jewellery, artworks, coins, stamps, and firearms. Nominal bits and pieces may be excluded. Furniture such as antiques bought from an accredited dealer may need to be appraised but if they are not particularly valuable, the executor may use two independent and impartial parties to certify a fair valuation of any specific items (the market value at the date of death). The market value is usually less than the insurance value.

High-end motor vehicles should be formally appraised. For all other motor vehicles, a valuation from a motor dealer is acceptable – either on their letterhead or on a rubber-stamped letter.

2. IMMOVABLE PROPERTY

The fair market value of immovable property is defined in the Estate Duty Act as the price which could be obtained on the sale of a property between a willing buyer and a willing seller in an open market.

With non-dutiable estates that have properties in urban and peri-urban areas, obtaining valuations from a local estate agent or using a municipal or local authority has become acceptable. A fair and accurate appraisement is particularly important when minors or redistributions are involved.

Revenue 246 from SARS is the prescribed form for the valuation of immovable property. The executor will need to complete the first page and send it to an appraiser for completion, together with a copy of the Letters of Executorship and title deed. The appraiser will charge a fee for the service.

The executor is also responsible for initiating, and seeing through to conclusion, the transfer of any inherited immovable property to a beneficiary. The transfer costs of a property that is not being sold will need to be included as a liability and reflected in the liquidation account. A pro forma account of transfer costs, certified by a conveyancer as being in accordance with the conveyancing fee guidelines of the Law Society in support of such costs, should be provided.

Estate duty on farms is calculated differently as certain concessions apply. It would be best for the executor to take specialist advice.

Should you own any property that is generating rental, the executor will have to collect the rentals once he/she has received his Letters of Executorship. The duties of the executor are to liquidate and distribute the estate. He/she has restricted contractual capacity and may not enter into a lease agreement on behalf of the estate – unless you give him/her authority in your Will. In practice, and for practical reasons, some executors do enter into lease agreements with the consent of the beneficiary or beneficiaries where it would benefit the estate.

3. FOREIGN ASSETS

The executor will have to communicate with the institutions holding the asset/s and establish their requirements. He/she may have to seek the services of a local specialist, as the institutions will require an authenticated copy of the death certificate, as well as court-certified copies of the Will and Letters of Executorship. Since the documents are going to a foreign country, they must be duly authenticated for use outside the Republic. Wills and Letters of Executorship are usually authenticated by the Master of the High Court under his hand and seal of office. Some countries may accept a notarially certified copy of a death certificate and other public documents as being sufficient, whilst other countries may require the notarial authentication to be further authenticated by the Registrar of the High Court. South Africa is a signatory to the Hague Convention. The Hague Convention designates each contracting state to appoint authorities to issue apostilles. Apostilles are generally used where both states are signatories to the Hague Convention. Embassies and consulates of certain countries prefer the use of Department of International Relations and Co-operation (DIRCO) apostilles.

4. LIABILITIES

All liabilities of the deceased estate as at the date of death must be disclosed in the Liquidation and Distribution account.

Essential services should be paid to avoid suspension. These payments may ultimately be refunded from the estate bank account. Liabilities that are neither funeral nor administration expenses require accurate vouchers clearly indicating that the liability existed at your date of death. Your executor should also include liabilities that he/she is expecting to fall due. Accurate vouchers must also be kept for funeral and administration expenses.

If you have signed surety for a third party, it will represent a contingent claim against your estate. Your executor should have a copy of the suretyship because he/she will need to find a way of either limiting further liability, or releasing your estate from liability altogether when you die. It must be sorted out as a matter of urgency.

*CLARIFICATION ON GROSS VALUE versus NET VALUE CALCULATION

The combined gross value of all property, both immovable and movable, and claims in favour of the estate, will determine the gross value of your estate. Once the executor has obtained all the necessary appraisements, the gross value can be calculated. The next step is to establish the net value by deducting all the legally allowable deductions. These include:

- Funeral and deathbed expenses. (Deathbed costs relate to medical expenses incurred prior to a person's death. It should be borne in mind that SARS has the finest tooth comb when it comes to claiming such deductions.)
- Costs of carrying out the Master's requirements.
- Liabilities as at date of death (this includes Income Tax and Estate Duty).
- Valuation fees on movable and immovable property.
- Estate administration costs.
- The value of usufruct or a limited right.
- Certain foreign property. (The claim depends on the deceased's residency status relative to how and when the foreign property was acquired.)
- Bequests to qualifying Public Benefit Organisations.
- Claims in terms of the Matrimonial Property Act.
- Fees on transfer of property (when immovable property is transferred to someone through inheritance, such transfer is exempt from transfer duty). On application, SARS will issue a transfer duty exemption certificate.
- Assets owned jointly by the deceased and a surviving spouse.

The process requires a methodical approach and meticulous record keeping.

MAIN POINTS:

- The executor should be thorough in the execution of his/her duty.
- He/she should err on the side of caution and consult the Master or a specialist if unsure about anything.

12.
HOW TO PROCEED ONCE THE LETTERS OF EXECUTORSHIP HAVE BEEN ISSUED

If the executor does not have the requisite expertise, he/she should appoint a specialist of choice to administer the estate (especially if the estate is complicated). Whoever is appointed is obliged to administer the estate under the supervision and authority of the Master. Every Master's office assigns a reference number to each deceased estate filed at his specific office. The numbers are allocated consecutively and independently of other offices. This number should be recorded and quoted in all correspondence with the Master.

Restriction:

- The sole representative of an estate may not leave South Africa for more than 60 (sixty) days without permission from the Master. If he/she has given Power of Attorney to an agent, it is less of an issue.

Alternative to appointing an agent:

- If he/she is reluctant to appoint an agent, plan B is "assumption". This avenue is open *providing your Will grants the executor the power of assumption.* The power of assumption in the Will allows him/her to co-opt another person to act as co-executor and share the workload, responsibility, and liability. The Deed of Assumption should be submitted by him/her to the Master, together with an Acceptance of Trust form completed by the co-executor to be appointed. If this co-executor is a parent, spouse or child of yours, a bond of security will not be required. At the same time, the executor will have to return his/her Letters of Executorship to the Master so that the document can be endorsed with the details of the co-executor and then returned to him/her.

To do:

- The Rev 267 form should be downloaded from the SARS website (https://www.sars.gov.za). It must be completed and is usually submitted with the Liquidation and Distribution account. It requires the executor/agent to record and calculate the estate duty payable on all assets identified in it. Knowing what SARS requires in due course should help the executor gather and collate all the necessary information early on and be ready when the time comes.
- Diarise the due date for the lodging of 1) the S 27 inventory (if ordered to do so by the Master, or where

security has been furnished); 2) the expiration dates of the notices published in the local newspaper and the *Government Gazette*; 3) the due date to lodge the Liquidation and Distribution account with the Master, and 4) the date on which the estate duty, if any, must be paid in order to avoid payment of interest. Estate duty is payable within 12 months from your date of death.

- File receipts for all estate-related expenditure.

PRIORITY #1: NOTICE TO CREDITORS AND DEBTORS

Placing the notice involves a cost (which changes from time to time).

The J193 form may be downloaded at https://justice.gov.za/master/forms.

Apart from placing the notice in the *Government Gazette*, the executor will also be required to place an advertisement in the local newspaper circulated in the area in which you ordinarily resided for the 12-month period prior to your demise.

The notice calls upon creditors who have a claim against your estate to lodge any such claims with the executor. The period allowed for creditors to lodge a claim is not less than 30 days, and not more than three months from the date of the latest publication of the notice. Executor's remuneration on gross income collected after date of death is calculated at 6%. It would therefore be beneficial for the executor to try and maximise the income collected after date of death.

The issue of solvency:

1. Solvent

Once the notice period has lapsed, the executor will be able to determine whether your estate is solvent – that is when the value of your assets exceeds the total amount of your liabilities. If your estate is solvent, he/she can proceed unhindered.

2. Insolvent

Section 34 of the Administration of Estates Act provides, inter alia, that on the expiry of the period specified in the notice referred to in section 29 (notice by creditors to lodge claims), the executor should satisfy him/herself as to the solvency of the estate. If the estate is found to be insolvent then, or at any time before distribution, he/she must forthwith by notice in writing (a copy of which notice is to be lodged with the Master), report the position of the estate to the creditors and inform them that unless the majority in number and value, or all the creditors, instruct him/her in writing within a stipulated period (being not less than 14 days), to surrender the estate under the Insolvency Act 1936, he/she will proceed to realise the assets in the estate in accordance with section 34(2) of the Administration of Estates Act. The administration of an insolvent deceased estate is complex, and the assistance of a specialist insolvency practitioner should be enlisted. It is beyond the scope of this book to discuss the administration of an insolvent deceased estate.

On smaller estates, the executor should approach the creditors him/herself for the purpose of negotiating a reduction in the value of their claims so that he/she can recover enough money to make up the difference. He/she will have to decide which of your assets should be sold to make up the deficit. He/she must also ensure that sufficient provision has been made for administration expenses and estate duty (if applicable). If he/she has appointed an agent, the agent will handle the negotiations.

How long does an executor have to lodge the liquidation and distribution account?
The account should be lodged within six months of the issue of his/her Letters of Executorship. For various reasons, this is not always possible. The executor may apply to the Master for an extension if he/she is unable to file the account in time. The Master will want to know why the account cannot be rendered in time, what measures have been taken to expedite the submission of the account, and what has been achieved to date. Repeated applications for an extension, without good cause, will not be entertained.

Similarly, your family and heirs will also expect regular progress updates – headway made, and snags under review. They may also have other concerns they would like to raise with the executor.

What if a beneficiary wants access to the inheritance before the estate has been wound up?
This is not an uncommon request. An executor does not have the authority to agree to such a request, since

the normal process requires the Master to examine and accept the Liquidation and Distribution account, and for such account to lie for inspection free from any objections. Any queries the Master may raise must be answered satisfactorily before the account may lie open for inspection. The account lies open for inspection for 21 days at the Master's office (only if the deceased was ordinarily resident in the area of the Master's office), and Magistrate's Court (if the deceased was not ordinarily resident in the area of the Master's office).

The executor may approach the Master for permission to release funds or property to a beneficiary before the estate has been formally wound up. Provided the estate is solvent and the beneficiaries are agreeable thereto, the executor will be inclined to release funds from the estate account to provide for the interim upkeep of your family or household and deduct these amounts when the final distribution takes place.

The balance of your estate's assets may only be distributed once all estate debt and tax liabilities have been paid in full, and SARS has issued the Deceased Estates Compliance Letter.

Updated Section 27 inventory (if applicable)
This is an updated inventory, after the one initially lodged with the reporting documents. Its purpose is to record any new or previously undisclosed asset/s that have since come to light.

PRIORITY #2: OPEN A DECEASED ESTATE BANK ACCOUNT

As soon as an executor has monies of R1 000,00 or more, he/she is required to open a deceased estate account in the name of the estate. Since different banks have varying criteria regarding the opening of the account, he/she should make a considered choice.

Hopefully, the executor will have all your banking information and be able to contact the bank/s regarding your death, arrange to open your deceased estate account and close the existing account/s. It would make sense to open the estate account at the same bank to facilitate the transfer of funds from the closed account/s to the estate account. Whilst banks differ on what additional documents they require to open the estate account, the executor should obtain originally certified copies as follows:

The deceased's:
- Death certificate
- National Identity Card/ Identity Document.

The executor's:
- Letters of Executorship/Authority
- National Identity Card/ Identity Document
- Proof of physical address.

If an agent is appointed, his/her:
- Power of Attorney (signed by the executor)
- National Identity Card/ Identity Document
- Proof of physical address.

While the estate bank statement will reflect all the activity on the account, the executor is responsible for all payments and withdrawals made from the estate account. A spreadsheet may help him/her identify and track transactions.

If there is a substantial amount of money in the estate account, he/she has an obligation to meet with the bank and explore better interest rate options. It would be advantageous to have a sum set aside should there be contingent or undetermined claims against the estate, or to make adequate provision for certain payments that are not immediately payable – like conveyancing costs, estate duty and administration costs. The current estate account should retain enough to cover more immediate expenses.

MAIN POINTS:

- Start as soon as the Letters of Executorship are issued.
- Be methodical and stay on top of the workload.
- Work closely with the family.

13.
THE ROLE OF A TESTAMENTARY TRUST

You have the option of establishing a testamentary trust in terms of your last Will and Testament. This is a legal mechanism used to protect vulnerable parties when you die. Minors or disabled beneficiaries qualify as vulnerable parties, and there are laws that protect them. Since you will no longer be around to personally manage and provide for their ongoing welfare, you need a framework through which you can pass the responsibility to people you trust. It is established in terms of a trust founder's last Will and Testament.

You may amend your testamentary trust during your lifetime, but once you die, the capacity to amend it is restricted. It is suggested that variations should be allowed, but limited to those of an administrative nature. Further, that the parameters be clearly identified by you when the trust is created, and that any variations permitted should be by trustee consensus. Under no circumstances is a testamentary trustee empowered to alter any beneficiaries' vested rights to trust benefits.

A living trust, by comparison, becomes operational on signature and may be amended by the trustees to accommodate changing circumstances and provide for generational longevity.

Here are some pertinent points to consider:

1. Statistically, women outlive men. What will happen to the assets you leave if your spouse remarries, and how might it affect the welfare of your children?

2. If you were to defy statistics and die young, how many of your beneficiaries could be minors (under the age of 18)?

3. On the untimely death of a spouse, the surviving spouse will have automatic custody and guardianship of their children. If there is no surviving spouse to care for the children, the Court will appoint a guardian and any bequests you have made to minors will be administered by the Guardian's Fund (currently overseen by the Public Investment Corporation). Interest earned on a bequest is released annually to the minor's legal guardian.

4. Immovable property registered in a minor's name may not be alienated or mortgaged, unless authorised by the Court or by the Master (where the value of such alienation or mortgage does not exceed R250 000,00). The provisions of Section 80 of the Administration of Estates Act are applicable.

What is a testamentary trust?

This trust form is created in your Will. Since its primary purpose is to protect your legacy and heirs, it should also give clear evidence that you intended to create a trust, which will require the skills of a specialist.

The framework of the trust should determine:

- How it should be set up and managed.
- The terms and conditions.
- Identify the property and assets to be awarded to the trust.
- Specify who the trust should protect (the beneficiaries, by name) and for how long.
- Nominate who you would like to act as trustees.

The beneficiaries own the assets as determined in your Will, and the trustees are appointed solely to manage them. It must be borne in mind that since the beneficiaries own the assets bequeathed to them, the door to creditors for any debt they incur is wide open.

A good trustee should:
- Be honest and have integrity.
- Understand finance.
- Know how to control and manage assets.
- Strive to create sufficient capital growth to offset the impact of inflation.
- Be familiar with tax law and know how to optimise tax efficiencies legally.
- Know how to manage people.

It is suggested that you have two or three trustees, one of whom should preferably be an independent trustee, as impartial opinion encourages balanced thinking.

Trust income may be used to ensure adequate maintenance for your spouse and children. If your spouse remarries, the funds held in trust for the children will be protected from the new spouse. Children from different relationships are also better protected.

The income tax applicable to testamentary trusts is the same as natural persons and based on the sliding scale of 18% to 45%, according to income tax brackets.

TYPES OF BENEFICIARIES TO CONSIDER

1. ***MINORS:***

   Their interests need to be safeguarded. Since they have no legal capacity according to South African law, they cannot manage assets or be party to a contract until they turn 18. The reasons for preferring trustees to manage the disbursement of trust funds are varied but they are legally obliged to adhere to your instructions; any additional expenditure requested is subject to their collective consideration. They are required to be objective and return a fair decision that does not pander to whim or waste.

   For tax purposes, the trustees may apply to SARS for the trust to be registered as a special trust type B because certain tax concessions apply. The conditions are that the minor is a blood relative of yours, is under 18 years of age and alive on the last day of February of the year of assessment.

   Immovable property left to a minor will be administered by his or her legal guardian.

2. ***DISABLED PARTIES:***

   Without special provision, individuals with diminished mental or physical capacity (unable to manage their own affairs or generate a life-sustaining income for themselves) may be left financially compromised and vulnerable. It could be that you have a disabled child, sibling or parent who requires financial support, someone you would like to continue providing for so that there is no compromise to the standard of care that they have been receiving.

Where the disability of a family member is permanent, the trustees may apply for a special trust type A (as determined in section 6B (1) of the Income Tax Act 58 of 1962) since it also offers some relief on Capital Gains Tax (levied at a maximum effective rate of 18% instead of 36%).

The Act defines a disability as "a moderate to severe limitation of any person's ability to function or perform daily activities because of a physical, sensory, communication, intellectual or mental impairment – on condition that the state of disability lasted or is likely to last for more than a year, and is diagnosed by a registered medical practitioner in accordance with the prescribed criteria".

3. *FINANCIALLY IRRESPONSIBLE PARTIES:*

Some beneficiaries need to be protected from themselves. They have either shown themselves to be irresponsible with money, or they lack the experience necessary to take care of substantial amounts of money. In the testamentary trust, you can stipulate at which age they may have full access to the inheritance you have left them. On reaching the age you determined, the trustees transfer the balance due to them.

A testamentary trust is also useful where an asset is not divisible and you would like all your heirs to derive either income or enjoyment from it, like a holiday home or a farm.

OTHER ASPECTS TO CONSIDER

The nominated trustees will have to apply to the Master of the High Court for their Letters of Authority. Without them, they do not have the authority to act. They are required to complete and submit to the Master an Application Form (J401), Acceptance of Trusteeship (J417), Acceptance of Auditor application (J405) and a beneficiary declaration (J450). The trustees must also lodge certified copies of their National Identity Card/ Identity Document and all the requirements listed on the JM21 memorandum.

A trust must be registered as a taxpayer and pay tax on retained income. Tax on distributed income is paid by the recipient. Financial statements must be drawn up and tax returns submitted annually.

MAIN POINTS:

- Testamentary trusts have their limitations, advantages, and disadvantages.
- Choose your trustees for their management and financial expertise.

14.
ESTATE TAXES

ESTATE DUTY

The Estate Duty Act 45 of 1955 governs the imposition, requirements, and parameters of estate duty. Estate duty is a death duty tax on the estate and anyone who accepts responsibility for the administration of a deceased estate should have a basic understanding of estate duty to perform his role effectively.

The Act imposes estate duty on the estate of every person who died on or after 1 April 1955. If your executor is expected to undertake this function himself and the complexity of your estate warrants it, he/she is advised to seek the services of a specialist.

A gross dutiable estate consists of:

- All property owned by a person at date of death, which includes the value of any fiduciary, usufructuary or any other like interest in property situate in the Republic, and the value of rights to certain annuities.
- All property deemed to be property of the person at date of death, which includes the proceeds of all domestic policies of insurance upon the life of the deceased, benefits due and payable from certain funds, the value of property donated in terms of section 56(1)(c) and (d) of the Income Tax Act and

property acquired by the deceased under section 3 of the Matrimonial Property Act, 1984. Section 56 of the Income Tax Act contains a list of exempt donations, which inter alia includes donations to approved Public Benefit Organisations, and donations made in contemplation of death (donation mortis causa).

All assets must be accounted for by the executor in the Liquidation and Distribution account. It requires the creation of a subsection for estate duty. The calculations that determine whether estate duty is payable are recorded in this section and if applicable, the amounts should be entered. The beneficiaries of insurance payments made directly to them may be called upon to contribute their respective proportionate share of the estate duty payable which is attributable to such payments.

The executor is also required to complete and submit the prescribed revenue form 267 from SARS, as it discloses detailed information about your property.

All returns are examined, and values allocated to estate assets carefully assessed. Section 5 of the Act stipulates how the property should be valued and what monetary value should be attached to a particular estate asset. The relevant authorities have the power to adjust values which are not in accordance with the provisions contained in section 5 of the Act. Section 74 of the Tax Administration Act empowers SARS to publish the names and particulars of individuals who have been convicted of certain offences related to estate duty. If the

Liquidation and Distribution account passes inspection by SARS and the final examination by the Master, he will allow the executor to lay it open for public inspection.

The executor is both responsible and accountable for the submission of the estate duty return and the payment of the estate duty assessment; SARS issues the assessment in the name of the estate. The executor may not pay any inheritances or legacies to beneficiaries until the estate duty is paid.

The application of estate duty:

- If you are ordinarily resident in South Africa and own property outside of South Africa, estate duty applies on your worldwide assets.
- If you are ordinarily resident in a different country, estate duty applies only on your South African assets.

What constitutes "property" in terms of a gross dutiable estate?

Basically, every asset included in the Liquidation and Distribution account, all fiduciary rights and usufructs vested in you as well as any annuities, are deemed to be property. When applied, allowable exclusions will reduce the amount payable from your estate.

Calculation of <u>gross value</u> of the estate:

1. All property of the deceased person as at date of death: Rxxx
2. Property deemed to be property of the estate at date of death: <u>Rxxx</u>
3. Gross value of the deceased estate (the sum of 1 and 2: Rxxx

Calculating the net value of the estate:

The <u>net</u> value of the estate is calculated by subtracting the deductions claimed in terms of section 4 and 4A of the Estate Duty Act from the gross value.

Once the net value is established, the primary rebate (usually referred to as the abatement) is deducted from such value to determine the dutiable amount.

Estate Duty is levied on the dutiable value of an estate at a rate of 20% on the first R30 million and at a rate of 25% on the dutiable value of the estate above R30 million. Section 4A of the Act provides for an abatement of R3 500 000 on deceased estates.

Examples:

<u>Deceased estate **A** has a net value of R5 000 000 (5 million) *before* the abatement is applied.</u>

R5 000 000 – R3 500 000 abatement = R1 500 000.

Estate duty at 20% of R1 500 000 = R300 000

<u>Deceased estate **B** has a net value of R29 000 000 (29 million) *before* the abatement is applied.</u>

R29 000 000 – R3 500 000 abatement = R25 500 000.

Estate duty at 20% of R25 500 000 = R5 100 000

<u>Deceased estate **C** has a net value of R50 000 000 (50 million) *before* the abatement is applied.</u>

R50 000 000 – R3 500 000 = R46 500 000

The first R30 000 000 is taxed at 20%.

(Tax payable = R6 000 000)

Balance of R16 500 000 is taxed at 25%.

(Tax payable = R4 125 000)

Total estate duty: R10 125 000.

Depending on the complexities of your estate (and

the conditions that apply to current, late, or previous spouses), the executor will probably need to consult a specialist.

ASSETS IN THE LIQUIDATION ACCOUNT

- Your "personal estate":
As already mentioned, when the executor calculates the estate duty, the values of the assets recorded in the liquidation account may be challenged by SARS. If SARS is not satisfied with the values provided, the executor will receive an order to adjust them.

  If an asset is sold out of the estate in the course of the liquidation of the estate and such sale is bona fide then the sale price becomes the value of the asset in the liquidation account. If shares in an unlisted company are sold the value is determined by an accountant or auditor, which value must be approved by SARS if there are estate duty consequences.

- Your fiduciary interests, usufructs, and other interests:
A fiduciary interest usually created in a Will or a trust deed refers to an interest by which property owned by a person (A), is bequeathed to another person (B) (fiduciary), subject to the condition that the property will pass to (C) (fideicommissary) on (B's) death. If (C) dies before (B) then (B) will obtain full dominium of the property. A usufructuary interest is also typically created in a Will or Trust Deed in terms of which a person (A) bequeaths the property

to another person (B), subject to the condition that another person (C) will have the benefit to use and enjoy the property and fruits thereof during his/her lifetime. Person (C) as usufructuary will never acquire ownership and dominium of the property.

- Annuities:

An annuity is identified as 1) being a fixed annual payment, even when divided into instalments, 2) payable annually for a period of more than a year, and 3) an obligation that is charged against property or a person and which is neither voluntary nor arbitrary. The estate duty obligations for each are different.

These applications are far from simple, they are fraught with extrapolated calculations and complex legal requirements that call for the services of a specialist.

- Life Insurance policies:

Life insurance policies are usually left to a beneficiary like a spouse, in which case they are paid directly to the designated beneficiary and the policy funds are not reflected as an asset in the Liquidation account. If you choose to take out the policy in your own name and appoint yourself as the beneficiary, the proceeds of the policy will be paid to the executor and the amount must be recorded as an asset in the Liquidation and Distribution account. Policies may also be ceded to institutions that are owed money – for example, to settle a mortgage bond with the bank.

The proceeds of all domestic life policies form part of the estate with two exceptions:

1. Proceeds paid to a spouse or child in terms of a registered antenuptial contract.
2. Certain business policies: for example, a policy whereby a business enterprise insures the life of a person who performs a valuable and specialised function in its service. Also, shareholder (or partnership) buy and sell policies are exempt. Special conditions apply to this type of policy if it is to be excluded from estate duty.

- Property bequeathed in a testamentary trust:
  Estate duty (if applicable) will first be subtracted from your estate before being transferred to the trust.
- Claims for accrual:
  If your marriage is subject to the accrual system in terms of the Matrimonial Property Act 88 of 1984, the executor will have to investigate claims for accrual between your estate and your surviving spouse. According to Section 3(1) of the Act, when a marriage is dissolved by death, the accrual implications must be investigated. It may be that an accrual claim in favour of the estate exists, in which case it is deemed to be property of the deceased.

This section is a user-friendly guide for the rooky executor who has been tasked with finalising a straightforward estate. Anyone who has wealth should appoint a specialist.

To everyone, rich or not, get your affairs in order!

And now that you have some insights into the complexity of winding up a deceased estate, the good news is that assets held in a Discretionary Living Trust avoid this entire rigmarole.

MAIN POINTS:

- An executor with no deceased estates experience should appoint a specialist as an agent.
- Ensure that allowable rebates are applied.
- Meet the submission deadlines.
- SARS has zero tolerance for non-compliance.

15.
HOW TO DETERMINE THE DEDUCTIONS AND REBATES APPLICABLE TO A DUTIABLE ESTATE

Once the executor has recorded all your assets in the Liquidation account and allocated fair values to them, he/she will be able to determine the gross value of your estate. Next is to establish what deductions and rebates apply.

DEDUCTIONS AND REBATES THAT ARE ALLOWED IN RESPECT OF A DECEASED'S GROSS PERSONAL ESTATE:

1. All reasonable deathbed and funeral expenses.
2. Administration costs to attend to the winding up of the estate (costs of advertising for debtors and creditors, Master's fee, valuation costs, cancellation, transfer and bond costs, bank charges etcetera).
3. Debts owed within South Africa, including any amount due to SARS in respect of tax liability to date of death.
4. Debts due by the deceased to someone resident in

another country. Approval from SARS is required.

5. The value of property accruing to a public benefit organisation or to entities that are exempt from tax, such as registered charities.

6. The value of any improvements made by a beneficiary (at his/her own expense during the deceased's lifetime and with the deceased's approval) by which the property has been enhanced by such improvements may be deducted from the gross value.

7. Bequests to a surviving spouse rank for a deduction to the extent of the amount received by the spouse.

8. The value of certain books and objects of art lent by the deceased to the state, a local authority, or certain other institutions for a period of 30 years or more, may be deducted.

9. The value of an asset situated in a foreign country which was acquired by the deceased *before* he or she relocated and became ordinarily resident in South Africa for the first time.

10. The value of an asset situated outside of South Africa that was acquired by the deceased through an inheritance or donation, made by someone who ordinarily resides in another country and is not ordinarily resident in South Africa.

11. Property situated outside of South Africa when it can be proven that it was acquired through the profits of the property described in 9 and 10.

12. An accrual claim by the surviving spouse against the deceased estate (see below).

MARRIAGE REGIMES:

- In Community of Property (determined by law).
  Your surviving spouse's half of the net joint estate is *not subject to estate duty* – this is applied only to the deceased's half of the estate. However, the deceased estate and the surviving spouse are *equally liable for estate debt.*

  Whilst *liabilities* against the joint estate are borne equally, funeral and deathbed expenses may only be applied to the deceased's portion of the estate.

- Antenuptial Contract
  The antenuptial contract must be scrutinised carefully to establish whether the marriage is subject to the accrual system or not. If the accrual system applies, then it is necessary to establish whether any assets have been excluded from the accrual system and how such accrual is to be calculated. An accrual claim which the surviving spouse has against the estate of the deceased is an estate liability and can be deducted from the gross estate. Where the estate of the deceased has an accrual claim against the surviving spouse, such accrual is deemed to be property in the deceased estate. Any amount which accrued to the estate by way of damages, other than damages for patrimonial financial loss and by inheritance or donation, is excluded. In order to calculate the accrual, it is necessary to establish the value of the deceased estate at the date of death and also the value of the estate of the surviving

spouse as at that date. The commencement values must be deducted therefrom. The total accrual must thereafter be divided by two. The party which has the lesser accrual will have a claim against the other for the difference.

Example:

	H	W
Net value at date of death	R700	R300
Less net commencement value (adjusted by weighted CPI)	R300	R200
Accrual	R400	R100
Total accrual for both estates	R500	
Accrual to each party	R250	
Accrual claim of wife against the deceased estate	R150	
	(R250-R100)	

Since South Africa has customary marriages or customary unions, an executor should have due regard to the nature and duration of the relationship between the deceased and such survivor when determining whether a claim applies. Constitutional issues may also have to be considered.

MAIN POINTS:

- The deceased's marriage regime and location of estate property influence the application of deductions and rebates.

16.
THE LIQUIDATION AND DISTRIBUTION ACCOUNT

Regulation 5(1) of the Regulations promulgated in terms of Section 103 of the Administration of Estates Act, 1965 prescribes how a liquidation and distribution account is to be drawn up. In view of its exceptional importance, the text of Regulation 5(1), updated 1988, is reproduced hereunder:

"Liquidation and Distribution Account

1. The account referred to in section 35(1) of the Act shall –

a. contain a heading which shall –

    i. describe it as a liquidation and distribution account;

    ii. reflect the ordinal number of such account;

    iii. specify whether it is a final or supplementary or an amended final or supplementary liquidation and distribution account, as the case may be;

    iv. state the full name and surname and date of death of the deceased, and, if an identity number was assigned to the deceased, such identity number also;

v. state the marital status of the deceased at the date of his death;

vi. if the deceased was a married person at the date of his/her death, state whether the marriage was in or out of community of property, and, if the marriage was in community of property, state the full name (including a maiden name, if applicable) of the person to whom he/she was so married, and, if an identity number has been assigned to that person, state such identity number also, and, if the marriage was out of community of property, state whether the marriage was subject to the accrual system in terms of section 2 of the Matrimonial Property Act, 1984 (Act 88 of 1984);

[Subpara. (vi) substituted by GN R2738 of 11 December 1987 (wef I February 1988).]

vii. specify, if adiation has taken place, that it is the massed estate of the deceased and the person who has so adiated; and

viii. state the Master's reference number;

b. contain a money column;

c. specify under a subheading "Liquidation account" –

i. the immovable property (other than property subject to a fideicommissum) forming part of the estate as described in the title deed thereof and reflect the number and date of the title deed and, in the case of an amended description of such property, also specify such amended description;

ii. an accurate and concise description of the movable property (not subject to a fideicommissum) forming part of the estate;

iii. in parentheses next to the money column of the account a consecutive number in respect of each item under this subheading, such number to correspond, where applicable, to the serial number of the voucher, receipt or acquittance referred to in sub-regulation (3), relating to such item;

iv. in the money column of the account, the value of each asset or a number of assets grouped together or the gross proceeds of each asset or a number of assets grouped together and sold by the executor;

v. the manner in which the executor intends dealing with or divesting the estate of any asset or group of assets, other than cash found in the estate or cash proceeds from assets realized,

and then the money column shall be totalled and thereafter the account shall, under this subheading, further specify -

vi. in the money column, the administration charges incurred in connection with the liquidation and distribution of the estate;

vii. the name of each creditor, together with the amount of his claim which shall be reflected in the money column of the account;

viii. in the money column, any estate duty payable by the estate,

and the amounts reflected in the money column in respect of subparagraphs (vi) to (viii), inclusive, shall be totalled and any balance for distribution to be carried forward to the distribution account shall be reflected in such column;

d. specify under a subheading "Recapitulation statement" a cash statement reflecting –

i. the total of the items comprising cash or property reduced to cash;

ii. the total debts and charges appearing under the subheading "Liquidation Account" and any legacy payable in cash; and

iii. the cash deficiency, if any, and how such deficiency will be settled;

e. specify under a subheading "Distribution account" –

i. the balance for distribution and particulars of any rights conferred under the provisions of section 37 of the Act;

ii. the full names of the heirs and whether an heir is a major or a minor, and in the case of –

a). a minor, also the date of birth, and if an identity number has been assigned to such a minor, also such identity number;

b). a woman, also her marital status and, if married in community of property, the full name of her husband and, if married out of community of property, whether the marital power has been excluded;

    iii.   briefly details of the property included in every award and the reason for every award and if the award to any beneficiary or administrator is subject to any condition in the will, stating that it is made subject to and in terms of such condition without specifying or summarizing the terms of the condition,

and where any redistribution agreement was entered into by the heirs and distribution has to be made by the executor pursuant to such agreement, the redistribution agreement shall accompany the account;

f.   specify under a subheading "Income and expenditure account" –

    i.   any income collected which has accrued subsequent to the death of the deceased to the date of the account;

    ii.   any expenses paid from such income;

    iii.   in parenthesis next to the money column of the account, a consecutive number in respect of each entry;

    iv.   the balance available for distribution and to whom it was awarded,

and if no income was collected, that fact shall be stated;

g.   specify under a subheading "Fiduciary Assets Account" –

    i.   *mutatis mutandis* in the manner set out in subparagraph (c) of this regulation, the fiduciary assets held by the deceased as a fiduciary pursuant to any will or other instrument;

ii. the origin of the fiduciary interest in such assets including the Master's reference number of the estate, will or instrument in terms of which such interest was created;

iii. any debts, charges and administration expenses which are chargeable against such fiduciary assets;

iv. in so far as the provisions of subparagraphs (*e*) and (*f*) of this regulation may be applied to the fiduciary assets account, the information required by those provisions;

h. where applicable, specify under a subheading "Estate duty" –

i. the calculations to establish whether estate duty is payable and the amount of estate duty payable, if any; and

ii. the apportionment thereof in respect of the persons liable for such duty in terms of the Estate Duty Act, 1955 (Act 45 of 1955);

i. conclude with a certificate signed and dated by the executor in which he/she –

i. declares that the account is to the best of his knowledge and belief a true and proper account of the liquidation and distribution of the estate;

ii. declares, if it is a final account, that to the best of his knowledge and belief all the assets and income collected subsequent to the death of the deceased to the date of the account have been disclosed therein; and

iii. sets forth, if the account is not a final account,

> full particulars of all the debts due to the estate and still outstanding and all assets, stating the approximate value of each asset, still unrealised with an explanation why such debts and assets have not been collected or realised."

The following is an example of a simple liquidation and distribution account.

In a nutshell, the liquidation account sets out the value of all property of the deceased and the value of all property deemed to be property of the deceased. The liability and administration expenses are deducted from the gross value to arrive at the net value of the estate. The dutiable amount is arrived at by deducting the rebate of R3 500 000,00 from the net value of the estate. The recapitulation statement reflects the property in the estate that has been reduced to cash; the legacies, if any, liabilities, and administration expenses, and whether there is a cash surplus or cash deficiency. The distribution account reflects the balance available for distribution, to whom such award/s is/are made and the causa for such award/s. This may be in terms of the Will of the deceased or in terms of intestate succession where the deceased did not leave a Will. The income and expenditure account refers to income accruing after date of death as well as expenditure after date of death. If a fiduciary interest was created, then this will be reflected in a fiduciary assets account, and finally there will be an estate duty account to determine whether there is any liability for estate duty.

A beneficiary is not compelled to accept any benefit under the Will or a benefit accruing in terms of the Intestate Succession Act No. 81/1987. He/she is entitled to renounce such benefit if he/she chooses to do so. Section 2C of the Wills Act 7 of 1953 provides that if any descendant of a testator, excluding a minor or a mentally ill descendent, who together with the surviving spouse of the testator is entitled to a benefit in terms of a Will, renounces his/her right to receive such a benefit, such benefit shall vest in the surviving spouse. Section 1 (6) of the Intestate Succession Act No.81 of 1987 provides that if a descendant of a deceased, excluding a minor or a mentally ill descendant, who together with the surviving spouse of the deceased, is entitled to a benefit from an intestate estate, renounces his/her right to receive such a benefit, such benefit shall vest in the surviving spouse. In certain instances, a benefit may be bequeathed to a beneficiary, subject to allowing his/her own property to devolve in terms of the Will. In other words, a bequest is made to a beneficiary with strings attached. The beneficiary has an election. He/she may adiate, in which case he/she is bound by the provisions of the Will, or he/she may repudiate. It often happens in practice that where parties are married in community of property and mass their estates, the surviving spouse sometimes elects to repudiate and take a one-half share of the joint estate by virtue of the marriage in community of property. The surviving spouse will, in those circumstances, not be entitled to the benefits under the Will.

MAIN POINTS:

- An executor needs to be skilled at crunching numbers and adept at bringing order to a complex process.

17.
MAKE ADEQUATE PROVISION FOR THE LESS OBVIOUS DETAILS

Pets may be less obvious, but they are equally important. Those loyal and trusted companions that have relied on you for love, protection, shelter, food and water, medical care, treats, walks, games, and a comfortable lap, are going to feel confused and bereft when you die. It would be a horrible injustice to overlook their continued welfare after you pass – for without a plan they may end up being surrendered to an animal shelter, or euthanased.

Pets are not assets that can be bequeathed. The responsibility for making proper provision for them rests with you while you are alive. The person you choose should be *willing and able* to take care of your pet. It means discussing it with the person ahead of time and securing his or her agreement.

Points to consider:
- Are they responsible, trustworthy, loving, and healthy enough to take care of your pet?
- Does your pet know and like them?
- Do they have the space to accommodate a pet?
- Are they permitted to keep pets where they live?

- Do they have the sort of facilities your pet is accustomed to, like a garden?
- What sort of adjustment might your pet have to make, like getting used to living with small children or other pets?
- Do they have allergies your pet may trigger?
- Are you planning to leave money in your estate for the upkeep of your pet?

It is difficult to estimate the lifespan of a pet and factor in the maintenance costs of food, veterinary bills, and possibly boarding from time to time.

A good way to make provision for your pet is to set up a testamentary trust which, as you know, will come into effect when you pass. Your intentions to create a trust must be made clear in your Will. In it, determine the amount of money you want set aside so that it can be transferred into the trust for safekeeping and distribution.

Discuss the trust with the trustees you have chosen, solicit their agreement and then appoint them in your Will. When you pass, the trust will be run as you determined.

The trustees will take their instructions from your Will and release the funds to the new carer as per your instructions (usually monthly). The carer may apply to the trustees for additional funds should extra be required to cover visits to the vet, medication or boarding in the carer's absence.

A clause regarding the termination of the trust

(usually on the passing of your pet) should be included, as well as an instruction regarding what to do with any residue of funds following the death of your pet. You may want to leave the residue to the carer, or a charity of choice.

MAIN POINTS:

- Do not abandon your pets and leave them at the mercy of people who do not want them.
- Choose replacement carer/s who can sustain the level of material, physical and emotional care to which your pet is accustomed.
- Make adequate material provision for their upkeep.

18.
HOW A DISCRETIONARY LIVING TRUST MAY BE OF BENEFIT TO A TESTATOR AND HIS BENEFICIARIES

Discretionary Living Trusts are fundamentally different from Testamentary Trusts. Testamentary Trusts are covered in chapter 13.

Compliance with the law – like the Trust Property Control Act 57 of 1988 and the recently amended Financial Intelligence Centre Act 38 of 2001 – remains the same.

The five key differences of a Discretionary Living Trust:

1. It is not Will-based or triggered by the founder's death.
2. The trust assets, beneficiaries and conditions are recorded in a trust deed, not the Will.
3. Ownership (without enjoyment) of trust assets is passed to the trustees, not the beneficiaries.

4. Trust assets may be preserved to secure generational wealth.
5. An executor is only required to wind up assets *outside* of the trust.

Why would a founder do this?

- So that the trust may become active and fully operational on signature.
- So that the founder may enjoy certain benefits from the trust during his/her lifetime.
- To facilitate succession planning with multi-generational benefits.
- To provide asset protection by thwarting irregular spending or attacks by third parties.
- To offer disability protection for the founder and avoid the possibility of curatorship.
- To accommodate changes to the trust deed, even after the founder's death.
- To enable property to be held in trust for minors or special needs individuals.
- To provide an income for beneficiaries during the founder's lifetime, and beyond.
- To operate a legitimate investment portfolio.
- To avoid having to wind up a deceased estate.
- To provide for tax-free distributions from the trust to heirs annually (within prescribed legal parameters).
- To get around having to pay estate duty and executor's fees.
- To allow for the uninterrupted flow of benefits to beneficiaries when the founder dies.

A founder's material legacy to his or her beneficiaries should not precipitate negative consequences for them, or him/herself. Consider this scenario:

Mr. X has three children. In his Will, he appoints his three children as beneficiaries, in equal shares. Mr. X will have created an estate for himself and one for each of his beneficiaries, which will ultimately, 1) incur estate administration charges (including executor's fees) for four estates, 2) each of the estates will be subject to the calculation of any applicable estate duty and capital gains tax and 3) have to be wound up according to the law, an exercise that can take anything from one to five years. Truth be told, there is no limit to the time it takes!

There may be costs associated with transferring assets into a Discretionary Living Trust, but these costs are outweighed by the costs of winding up multiple estates. When compared, it is suggested that the costs saved from setting up a Discretionary Living Trust in his lifetime will benefit Mr. X, his immediate beneficiaries, and future generations. Also, assets distributed through a trust avoid the inevitable, indeterminate delays and frustration associated with winding up an estate.

Every Discretionary Living Trust deed is unique to the client. The terms, conditions and details of each trust are nuanced by the circumstances and objectives of the founder. It gives the trustees all the information and powers they need to carry out their duties efficiently and remain accountable to the law, to each other and to the beneficiaries.

MAIN POINTS:

- Since trusts are complex legal entities with multiple benefits and certain disadvantages, be sure to explore the possibilities and parameters with a specialist.
- Discretionary Living Trusts allow for greater flexibility with potential tax-saving benefits.
- Choose trustees with integrity and financial nous.
- Avoid creating multiple estates.

19.
HOW TO DEAL WITH ASSETS IN SEVERAL DIFFERENT COUNTRIES

Estate duty is applied to a deceased person's worldwide assets.

Global financial markets have become increasingly accessible over the years and many South Africans are opting to include offshore investments as a component of their investment portfolios. They are an option to be explored under the guidance of a specialist.

As with most investment opportunities, there are potential risks and considerations that must be borne in mind. One of the risks may be your executor. How familiar is he/she or she with international law and global financial markets?

Basically, two law systems apply globally – civil law and common law. They are adapted by each country to accommodate their specific circumstances, metamorphous changes, and culture.

1. Civil law is more systemised and prescriptive, with codified statutes. Typically, the specific codes of the country are recorded in their constitution, so the constitution provides the framework for legal matters.

2. Common law is based on precedential opinion, a system by which lawyers argue a case before a judge. Their arguments are guided by the evolution of judicial opinion. Modified over centuries as different legal situations arose, the historical accumulation of decisions has become the basis for common law. This allows for greater freedom of contract.

(Freedom of contract is described by Merriam Webster as "a power or right to contract, and freely determine, the provisions of contracts without arbitrary or unreasonable legal restrictions".)

The South African legal system is based on common law (Roman Dutch in origin) and supplemented by legislation. International law is a minefield, especially for an executor. When you consider that offshore assets will be subject to the foreign investment laws of each country, and those laws may even take precedence over the provisions of your Will, you will begin to appreciate the complexity of offshore investing and the ramifications for the executor.

How are these assets realised, or passed to your heirs when you die? Some countries have replaced freedom of testation with mandatory succession laws. Be sure you understand the rules and limitations imposed by the host country so that when you die, your offshore assets pass to your heirs as you envisioned.

Should you have a separate Will for your foreign assets? If you choose this option, get advice from a specialist in the relevant jurisdiction and have the Will structured to conform to that country's regulations. A South African specialist can assist up to a point, but he or she is unlikely to know the requirements of other jurisdictions well enough.

Financial and other implications:

- Offshore assets in your name must be included in your deceased estate in South Africa and will be included in your estate duty and capital gains tax calculations.
- Ownership of assets in some foreign countries may incur a death duty liability according to their own laws (which could result in double death duty liability). Double taxation will significantly complicate the winding up of your estate and incur taxes you had not anticipated. There may, however, be relevant treaties in place which will avoid the problem of double tax.
- The transfer of assets into a beneficiary's name will also be subject to the laws of the host country.
- Offshore assets will be subject to exchange control regulations.
- If you have a Will in South Africa and another in the asset host country, it is important that they are aligned. They should never contradict, supersede, replace, or unintentionally revoke one another.
- They must be properly worded to avoid confusion. The nuances of technical terms in another language may be very difficult to translate.
- If you create a property portfolio as an investment, you will find that succession to land may be highly

> regulated by the jurisdiction in which the land is located.

- Foreign countries often have different marital rights and varying determinations of adulthood.

Also, the Letters of Executorship issued in South Africa may not be recognised by the authorities and administrator of your offshore assets. If there is no offshore Will, the executor must ensure that all the official death documents are properly formalised and apostilled by the Master before sending them to any foreign executor. (Apostilled refers to a certificate of authentication to legalise a document for use in another country.)

The documents may have to be translated before sending them to the foreign authorities for reporting purposes. The phrasing and wording run the risk of being lost in translation and muddying the waters, which will incur further costs, precipitate delays, and create a serious hurdle for the executor.

Offshore assets are a positive investment platform when all aspects are carefully considered and imple-mented advisedly. They allow for a globally diversified portfolio across countries, asset classes and currencies. Specialists advise that they should be driven more by long-term investment goals and the desire to spread your investment risk, and less by a knee-jerk reaction to South Africa's volatile socio-economic climate.

All these matters must be dealt with by the executor, and the support of a specialist is warranted.

MAIN POINTS:

- Get the right advice from a specialist at the outset.
- Investigate how the investments will impact the winding up of your estate and what measures may be taken to overcome potential complications for the executor.
- Steer clear of emotional decisions based on the prevailing political sentiment.

20.
LIFE INSURANCE

Life insurance is a brilliant estate planning instrument, but the need for it should be objectively determined. It is often applied to manage risk, and since it may and is usually paid directly to the beneficiary (usually a spouse) it provides necessary liquidity when a family breadwinner dies. The liquidity should be sufficient to cover a family's needs while the estate is being wound up as well as settle any estate taxes payable.

When the owner of a domestic life insurance policy dies, someone should inform the insurance company, usually the insurance broker or beneficiary. The company will request certain documents including an originally certified copy of the death certificate before releasing any funds. If the insurer requires any other documents, they must be supplied.

Regardless of who or what has been named as the beneficiary of the policy, the executor must reflect the full proceeds of the life insurance payout as a deemed asset in the Estate Duty section of the Liquidation and Distribution account. Even if the policy has been ceded as security for a debt owing, it must reflect in the Estate Duty section of the Liquidation and Distribution account and the debt amount due as a deduction.

If the surviving spouse/life partner is the beneficiary

of the life insurance policy, the amount paid out is exempt from estate duty. Similarly, estate duty will not apply if the life policy is registered under a duly recorded antenuptial or postnuptial contract and the contract clearly stipulates a spouse or child as the nominated beneficiary of the policy.

If a beneficiary has not been nominated in the policy, the funds will be paid into the estate. If there is a Will and the estate is the beneficiary of the policy, it will devolve according to the Will. If there is no Will, it will be subject to intestate succession laws.

Life insurance is a deemed asset for estate duty calculation, regardless of who the beneficiary is. If the estate is the beneficiary of the life insurance, executor fees will apply.

When you die, a priority on the executor's "To Do" list will be to carry out an analysis of the available liquidity in your estate – cash and investments, life insurance and any inheritance contributions payable by heirs. Then he/she needs to calculate the cash required to settle the estate liabilities, executor's fees, Master's fees, funeral expenses, taxes (income and capital gains tax), estate duty and cash bequests. Once both sections have been analysed and calculated, he/she will have a better idea of what is due and recoverable and whether it constitutes a surplus or a shortfall. If it is the latter, he/she may have to sell assets to recover the shortfall.

Important points for you (testator) and your executor to discuss ahead of time, and update as circumstances change:

- If you have life insurance, discuss the insured amount with your executor and to whom the proceeds will be payable when you pass.
- Create a list for the executor of all the liabilities that currently exist. Discuss how they might be reduced before you die.
- Talk about what the executor should do if your life insurance is insufficient to provide the necessary liquidity to pay the relevant death taxes and/or any outstanding debt.
- Check whether your life insurance policy has been reviewed and/or updated to meet any changes in circumstances. For instance, is your ex-spouse still the main beneficiary of the policy?
- Inform the executor about the possible effect your marriage regime may have on your life insurance policy.
- Your executor should know about any measures you have taken to mitigate the effect of estate duty and capital gains tax.
- If the beneficiaries of the life insurance policy are still minors (under 18) when you pass, discuss how this will impact your plans and what the executor should do.
- If a trust is to receive the proceeds of the life insurance, discuss the details with him/her.

The executor will manage your deceased estate so much more efficiently if he/she is fully appraised of every component within it. It will help in handling any curve balls that may disrupt the process. Liquidity will also be required quite urgently when you pass. Treat it as a priority while you can, and investigate options like life insurance, if necessary.

MAIN POINTS:
- When you die, provision for ongoing family maintenance costs will require urgent liquidity.
- Avoid nominating the estate as the beneficiary.
- Explore your options and decide which will best meet your family's financial obligations in the short and medium term.
- The pay-out made to a policy beneficiary (other than the estate) will not be managed by the executor.

SUMMARY

Most people believe they have plenty of time to get their affairs in order, and most do. The "I'm going to live for ever" excuse has been disproven for millennia. The wisdom of, and commitment to, advance planning for the inevitable will greatly facilitate a smoother transition for those we love once we are gone.

A life-threatening situation should never be the trigger. Rushing something as important as a Will may lead to omissions and have a significant bearing on your intentions. Why wait for a life-changing event (or old age, for that matter) to sort out your affairs and record your final wishes?

Similarly, bear in mind that a Will should be drafted – preferably professionally – and signed by the testator/testatrix before he or she experiences any loss of mental capacity. If you compel or coerce a mentally incapacitated person to sign any legal document they do not understand, it is automatically rendered invalid.

The reality of our times compels us to think ahead. Planning early creates the assurance that the disposal of our assets will be carried out as we intended, without unnecessary delays, consequences, or disruption to the financial support of our loved ones.

To create a Will a person must be at least 16 (sixteen) years old and capable of appreciating the nature and effect of the act. A Will can be amended by executing a Codicil to accommodate any changes during your lifetime. The same requirements apply for a Codicil as for a Will.

Treat the creation of a Will as one of life's imperatives. I urge you not to die intestate. The consequences for your loved ones will be challenging, possibly divisive and unkind.

Be sure to nominate an executor in your Will, the person who will be entrusted with the winding up of your estate. This trustworthy confidant should be privy to your plans before you die, and also someone who can be relied upon to carry out your wishes with a high degree of competence – made possible because he or she already has the necessary in-depth knowledge of your estate (its assets and liabilities, your heirs, and intentions).

This book has carefully detailed the complex preparation (by the testator/testatrix) , implementation challenges (for the executor), and process of winding up a deceased estate (the legal requirements). It is not a simple task: all parties must appreciate the magnitude and scope of work involved.

The length of time it takes to wind up an estate has long concerned me. Delays have the potential to cause needless hardship for your heirs, especially if you have not made provision for their immediate needs.

In my previous book, *Estate Planning Trusts for Everyone – Discretionary Living Trusts – A Legacy for Generations*, I cover the merits of an estate plan that utilises a Discretionary Living Trust to provide for asset protection, succession planning and disability protection.

Assets held in a trust circumvent the protracted process of winding up a deceased estate and save both executor fees and estate duty. Most importantly, it also ensures that there will be no interruption to the flow of benefits to your beneficiaries when you die.

Get your affairs in order and ensure that every element of your personal and financial matters is clear and tidy. Consult a specialist to draft your Will and estate plan so that nothing is ambiguous, overlooked, or left to chance. Any legal challenges that arise from a poorly drafted Will are going to incur hefty legal costs, and potentially create conflict among your loved ones.

This book not only provides recommended reading for professionals such as Attorneys, Accountants, Fiduciary Practitioners and Administrators, it serves as a useful guide for members of the public and students who require information relevant to Estates and Trusts.

My masterful grasp on the complexity of Deceased Estates and Trusts is widely recognised.

Estate Planning Trusts for Everyone – Discretionary Living Trusts – A Legacy for Generations is also available at select bookstores nationwide or from Porcupine Press.

To get in touch with me, go to www.mmtrustspecialist. co.za.

GLOSSARY

ADIATION: The acceptance of a benefit under a Will.

ASSET: Owned property of value.

BENEFICIARY: A general term for anyone who receives assets or benefits from a benefactor.

CLOSE CORPORATION: A legal entity that has no share capital and no shareholders. The owners are known as members and their interest is expressed as a percentage. For tax purposes, it is treated like a company.

CODICIL: An alteration to the Will.

CREDITOR: A person or company to whom money is owed.

DEBTOR: A person or company that owes money.

DEEMED ASSET: Property that comes into existence as the result of a person's death. It is important that this be included for the calculation of estate duty in the Liquidation and Distribution account.

DEVOLVE: To pass on (something such as responsibility, rights, or powers) from one person, or entity, to another.

ESTATE: Every tangible and intangible asset that makes up the *net worth* (assets minus liabilities) of an individual – from property and investments to belongings, cash, and collectibles, which they had as at date of death.

GUARDIANSHIP: When parental responsibilities and rights are bestowed on a third party, either in terms of a Will or by a court of law. These relate to the control and administration of the child's estate, the responsibility to safeguard the child's property and property interests, the capacity to assist or represent him or her in administrative, contractual, and other legal matters, and to give or refuse consent required by law in respect of matters concerning the child. The Children's Act 2005 has since introduced the concept of "care" to guardianship, such as the responsibility to protect and uphold the child's right to an acceptable standard of living in terms of it being conducive to his or her health, wellbeing and development.

HEIR: A beneficiary designated in the Will to receive a pre-determined portion of the residue of the estate, that is, what is left after all relevant taxes and creditors have been paid and legatees have received their legacy.

LEGATEE: A beneficiary designated in the Will to receive something specific.

LIABILITY: The state of being legally responsible for something.

LIFE INSURANCE: Also known as "whole life cover", has no fixed expiry date, covers the policyholder for his or her entire life (providing all premiums are up to date) and payout is assured upon death.

LIQUIDATION: The process of selling off assets and using the proceeds to pay off creditors and shareholders.

MASTER: The Master of the High Court.

REPUDIATION: The rejection of a benefit under a Will.

TESTAMENTARY: Relating to or bequeathed or appointed through a Will.

TESTATOR (male): One who makes or has made a valid Will; one who dies leaving a valid Will.

TESTATRIX (female): As above.

TRUSTEE: An individual person or member of a board given control or powers of administration of property in trust with a legal obligation to administer solely for the purposes specified.

WILL: Also known as a *Testament*, a written document in which a person voluntarily sets out, in precise and unmistakable terms, what must happen to his or her estate when he or she dies.

APPENDIX

Rev16   Claim for refund out of revenue

Rev246   Valuation of immovable property

Rev267   Return of information required in terms of section 7 of the estate duty act, Act 45 of 1955

Rev268   Estate duty return of claims paid under policies of insurance which are "Domestic policies" upon the life of a deceased person

J155

REPUBLIC OF SOUTH AFRICA

UNDERTAKING AND ACCEPTANCE OF MASTER'S DIRECTIONS
BY EXECUTOR/EXECUTRIX
[SECTION. 18 (3), ACT No. 66 OF 1965

ESTATE No. ....

1. Estate late ....

   (Full names and surname)

   ....

   died on .... Identity number

2. District where deceased was residing ....

3. Full names of applicant ....

   Identity number   *A certified copy of the applicant's Identity Document must accompany this form*

4. Relationship to deceased ....

5. Residential address .... Postal address ....

   ....

   ....

Telephone number (Home) .... - .... Telephone number (Work) .... - ....

6. Name and postal address of agent (if applicable) ....

.... Telephone number .... - ....

7. I undertake to administer the estate, to pay the debts from the estate assets and to distribute any balance according to the Master's directions in terms of section 18 (3) of the Estates Act, 1965, and accept that I am bound by any amendment or cancellation of such directions.

8. I undertake that I shall not administer any asset(s) which has/have not been reflected in the section 9 inventory, and as soon as it becomes known to me that the value of the assets exceed R250 000 to report to the Master this fact. and to return the directions.

9. I confirm that to the best of my knowledge the estate is solvent and undertake to immediately advise the Master when it becomes known to me that the estate is insolvent. That to my knowledge the known liability/ies of the estate is/are as follows:

....

....

....

....

10. I hereby declare that I am not an unrehabilitated insolvent.

Signed on ....
(Date)

....
Signature of applicant

....
PRINT NAME AND SURNAME

G.P.-S. 003-0317

J170

REPUBLIC OF SOUTH AFRICA

MAGTIGINGSBRIEF
LETTERS OF AUTHORITY

[Artikel 18(3) van die Boedelwet, No, 66 van 1965 (soos gewysig)]
[Section 18(3) of the Administration of Estates Act, No. 66 of 1965 (as amended)]

No: ....

HIERBY WORD GESERTIFISEER dat
THIS IS TO CERTIFY that

....

ID: ....

behoorlik gemagtig word om die bates in die Boedel wyle
has/have been duly authorized to take control of the assets of the Estate of the late

....

Identiteits No:
Identity No: ....

wie oorlede is op
who died on: ....

soos in die inventaris by my ingedien, vermeld, onder beheer te neem, die boedelskulde te vereffen en eiendomsreg van die restant aan die erfgenaam/erfgename ingevolge die geldende reg oor te dra.

As reflected in the inventory filed with me, to pay the debts, and to transfer the residue of the estate to the heir/heirs entitled thereto by law.

BATE(S) / ASSETS	BEDRAG/AMOUNT
	R

....

Meester van die Hooggeregshof
Master of the High Court

PS/NS:
Waar vaste eiendom betrokke is, moet in gedagte gehou word dat oordrag daarvan in die Akteskantoor geregistreer moet word. Vuurwapens moet gelisensieer word.
In cases involving immovable property, it must be borne in mind that transfer thereof must be registered in the Deeds Office. Firearms must be properly licenced.

DATUMSTEMPEL
DATE STAMP

FORM J187

REPUBLIC OF SOUTH AFRICA

LIQUIDATION AND DISTRIBUTION ACCOUNTS IN DECEASED ESTATES LYING FOR INSPECTION

In terms of section 35 (5) of the Administration of Estates Act, No. 66 of 1965, notice is hereby given that copies of the liquidation and distribution accounts (first and final, unless otherwise stated) in the estates specified below will be open for the inspection of all persons with an interest therein for a period of 21 days (or shorter or longer if specially stated) from the date specified or from the date of publication hereof, whichever may be the later, and at the offices of the Masters of the High Court and Magistrates as stated. Should no objection thereto be lodged with the Masters concerned during the specified period, the executors will proceed to make payments in accordance with the accounts.

* **Mandatory Fields / Verpligte Velde**

*Notice Language:
Taal van kennisgewing:

English #   Afrikaans #

*Province:
Provinsie:

Province of the Master's office specified on this form.
Provinsie van die Meesterskantoor gemeld op hierdie vorm.

A.   *Estate Number:
Boedelnommer:

*Surname / Van:

*First Names / Voorname:

South African
ID Number:

OR

Passport /
Other ID:

*Last Address / Laaste Adres:

**B. Complete this section only if deceased was married in community of property /
Voltooi hierdie gedeelte slegs as oorledene binne gemeenskap van goedere getroud was**

First Names of Surviving Spouse / Voorname van Nagelate Eggenoot(note):

Surname of Surviving Spouse / Familienaam van Nagelate Eggenoot(note):

ID Number of Surviving Spouse / ID Nommer van Nagelate Eggenoot(note):

C. Description of Account if other than First and Final:
Beskrywing van rekening **indien anders as Eerste en Finale is:**

Period of Inspection (if other than 21 days):
Tydperk van Insae (indien korter of langer as 21 dae):
Magistrate's Office / Landdroskantoor:

Master's Office / Meesterskantoor:

---

*Advertiser Name:

Advertiser Address:

Advertiser Email:

*Date Submitted: *Advertiser Telephone:

***For Publication in the Government Gazette on:**   (CCYY-MM-DD)
Vir Publikasie in die Staatskoerant op:

J190

REPUBLIC OF SOUTH AFRICA

ACCEPTANCE OF TRUST AS EXECUTOR

Complete in duplicate

Estate No. ....

A.   I (full names and surname) ....

Residential address... Business address..

....

....

....

Telephone number(s) .... Telephone number(s) ....

....

Identity No.   .... Relationship to deceased..

(An originally certified copy of the applicant's Identity Document must accompany this form)

hereby apply for appointment as Executor in the estate of:

Full names and surname..

Date of birth .... Date of death ....

Identity No. .... Income tax ref. No..

District in which deceased normally resided...

Name of surviving spouse

....

B. For the purpose of this executorship I declare the following:

- I choose *domicilium citandi et executandi* for the purpose of service of process of court, writs of execution and the receipt of all notices contemplated in the Administration of Estates Act, No. 66 of 1965 (as amended), at (not P.O. Box number):

  ....

- I understand the duties and penalties applying to the office of Executor which have been explained to me.

- I am not an unrehabilitated insolvent. Nor have I at any time committed an act of insolvency. [Note section 8 of the Insolvency Act, No. 24 of 1936 (as amended)].

- A Bond of Security to the value of **R**.. for the full value of the estate is attached.

- I am exempt from furnishing security.

- I am permanently residing in the Republic of South Africa, and I undertake to advise the Master of the High Court immediately should my estate or that of a person who has signed as surety for the Bond of Security be sequestrated, or commit an act of insolvency, or should I proceed to reside outside the Republic of South Africa.

- The name and address of my agent is.................................. ....

  ....

- I fully understand that my appointment of an agent does not release me from my responsibilities as required by law.

C. Signed at..on .... year ....

....
    Applicant Name and Surname   ***Applicant Signature***

GP-S 81/811521

J192
(81/811521)

REPUBLIC OF SOUTH AFRICA

AFFIDAVIT

PARTICULARS OF NEXT-OF-KIN

I, ...

of...

....

*do hereby make oath and say/affirm that within is a true and complete statement of the next-of-kin of the deceased, and I make this statement conscientiously, believing the same to be true.

....
Signature   *Print Name and Surname*

Signed and *sworn to/affirmed before me

at..

this............................... day of... in the year.

The deponent has acknowledged that he/she knows and understands the contents of this affidavit and adheres to it.

....
*Magistrate/Justice of the Peace/Commissioner of Oaths

Area for which appointed ....

If appointment is held ex officio, state office held.......... ....

* Delete if not applicable.

J192

* Separate affidavits in respect of each predeceased child must be completed.

Names and addresses of the next-of-kin of the late...

who died at... on ....
(Place) (Date)

N.B.:   The date of death is to be inserted opposite the name of any deceased relative. Against those degrees of relationship in which the deceased never had any relative, the word "NONE" is to be inserted.

Relatives to be accounted	Names of relatives and degree of relationship
1. Surviving spouse:	
2. Children and date of their birth. Also state names of *predeceased children and their dates of death:	
Ignore questions 3, 4 and 5 if the deceased left children or descendants.	

3. Father of deceased: Mother of deceased:	
Ignore questions 4 and 5 if the parents are both alive. 4 Brothers and sisters of the deceased. State whether full or half blood, and their addresses and dates of birth. State the name of the step-parent of half brothers and half sisters:	
5. Names of brothers and sisters who are dead, date of deaths, and names, addresses and dates of birth of their children, if any	

FORM J 193

REPUBLIC OF SOUTH AFRICA

NOTICE TO CREDITORS IN DECEASED ESTATES

All persons having claims against the under-mentioned estate must lodge it with the Executor concerned within 30 days (or as indicated) from date of publication hereof.

*** Mandatory Fields / Verpligte Velde**

*Notice Language:
Taal van kennisgewing: English #   Afrikaans #

*Province:
Provinsie:

Province of the Master's office specified on this form.
Provinsie van die Meesterskantoor gemeld op hierdie vorm.

A.   *Estate Number:
Boedelnommer:

*Surname / Van:

*First Names / Voorname:

*Date of Birth:
Geboortedatum: (ccyy-mm-dd)

*ID Number:
ID Nommer:

*Last Address / Laaste Adres:

*Date of Death:
Datum van Oorlye: (ccyy-mm-dd)

Master's Office / Meesterskantoor:

B. Only applicable if deceased was married in community of property/subject to the accrual system:

First Names of Surviving Spouse / Voorname van Nagelate Eggenoot(note):

Surname of Surviving Spouse / Familienaam van Nagelate Eggenoot(note):

Date of Birth of Surviving Spouse / Geboortedatum van Nagelate Eggenoot(note): (ccyy-mm-dd)

ID Number of Surviving Spouse / ID Nommer van Nagelate Eggenoot(note):

C. *Name of Executor or Authorised Agent / Naam van Eksekuteur of Gemagtigde Agent:

*Address of Executor or Authorised Agent / Adres van Eksekuteur of Gemagtigde Agent:

D. Period allowed for lodgement of claims, **if other than 30 days**:
Tydperk toegelaat vir lewering van vorderings **indien anders as 30 dae**:

*Advertiser Name:

Advertiser Address:

Advertiser Email:

*Date Submitted: *Advertiser Telephone:

G.P.-S. 003-0318

J243

REPUBLIC OF SOUTH AFRICA

INVENTORY

In terms of section *9 (1) (a)/9 (2) (a)/9 (2) (b)/27/78 of the Administration of Estates Act, 1965.

Attention is directed to the provisions of section 102 (1) (b) of the Act which provides that any person who wilfully makes any false inventory under the Act shall be guilty of an offence and liable on conviction to a fine not exceeding R1 000 or to imprisonment for a period not exceeding five years or to both such fine and such imprisonment.

* Full name of deceased ....

Full name of surviving spouse (in a case where spouses were married in community of property)

....

Address of surviving spouse

....

Massed estate of ....

of/or

* Full name(s) of minor(s) under tutorship or person in respect of whose property letters of curatorship have been granted:

....

Full address ....

I(full name) ....

of (full address) ....

in my capacity as..

hereby declare that to the best of my knowledge and belief the with-in mentioned is a true and correct inventory—

* (a) of all property known to me to have belonged, at the time of death, to the *above-named deceased/joint estate of the above-named deceased and surviving spouse/above-named massed estate;

* (b) of all property known to me to have been in the possession of the above-named deceased upon the premises at

....at the time of *his/her death;

* (c) showing the value of all property in the above-named estate;

* (d) of all the property taken care of or administered by me.

....
        Place   Date   Signature

                                                          ....
                                                          Print Name and Surname

Names and addresses of persons having an interest in the estate as heirs in whose presence this inventory was made. (To be furnished in the case of an inventory under section 9 of the Act):

....

....

....

1. Immovable property

Description of property according to the title deed (also state number and date thereof)	Value	
	R	c

Total .... R 0.00

2. Movable property

Description	Value	
	R	c

173

Total .... R	0.00

3. Claims in favour of estate

Description	Value	
	R	c

Total .... R | 0

SUMMARY

		R	c
1.	Immovable property	0	
2.	Movable property	0	
3.	Claims in favour of estate	0	
	Total .... R	**0**	

G P-S 81/814652

J262
(81/814652)

REPUBLIC OF SOUTH AFRICA

Administration of Estates Act,
No.66 of 1965 (as amended)

UNDERTAKING AND BOND OF SECURITY
by INTERIM CURATOR / EXECUTOR / FOREIGN EXECUTOR / TUTOR / CURATOR

In the estate of...

I / We ....

[Full name(s)]

of...

....

[Full residential and business address(es)]

do hereby undertake and bind myself / ourselves jointly and severally, should I / we be appointed by the Master of the

High Court (.. Division) to administer the above estate and/or liquidate and distribute

the assets thereof as INTERIM CURATOR(S) and/or EXECUTOR(S) or FOREIGN EXECUTOR(S) or TUTOR(S) or

CURATOR(S) properly according to law and to pay to the Master of the High Court ....

Division) on demand an amount up to R .... (...rand) as the

Master may claim from me/us in respect of any loss or damage as may be suffered by the said estate or by the minor(s)

or person under curatorship of by any other person by reason of the fact that I/we failed to perform properly my/our functions in the above capacities or because of any maladministration on my/our part.

A certificate under the hand of the Master or his duly authorized representative to the effect that I/we failed to discharge my/our functions as aforesaid and stating the amount of such loss or damage shall be accepted as *prima facie* proof of such failure and of the extent of such loss or damage.

I / we choose as my/our *domicilium citandi et executandi* and for the purpose of the service of any notices or for the service of any legal process:

....
(Not a post box number)

SIGNED at.. on..
(place)   (date)

AS WITNESSES:

1. ....   1. ....

2. ....   2. ....
Signature(s)
(a woman married in community of property or without exlusuion of marital power, must be assisted by her husband).

AS WITNESSES: ASSISTED BY:

1. ....   1. ....
(HUSBAND)

2. ....

SURETYSHIP
by INSURANCE COMPANY/BANK/FINANCIAL INSTITUTION

I/We, ...

in my/our capacity as...

of the...

my/our principal do hereby interpose and bind my/our principal as surety and co-principal debtor *in solidum*, jointly and severally with

....

[hereinafter referred to as the Incumbent(s)] unto and in favour of the Master of the High Court

(.. Provincial Division) ("the Master")

for the due and proper performance by the incumbent(s) of his/their duties/functions in the aforesaid office(s) and the proper

administration of, and accounting by him/them for all funds and property of the Estate/Company/Trust under his/their administration as

required by law and in default thereof to pay to the Master on demand an amount up to the sum of R..

(.. rand) as the Master may claim from my/our principal

in respect of such loss or damage as may be suffered by the Estate / Company / Trust ór any person by reason of such default.

Provided that:
1.   My/Our principal's liability hereunder will not exceed the sum of R ....(.. Rand);

2.   (a)   in the event of any alleged default on the part of the incumbent(s) in his/their aforesaid office, giving rise to an alleged
claim under this suretyship, my/our principal will be notified by the Master in writing of the alleged default and the amount of the alleged
loss or damage suffered, which notification shall be *prima facie* of such default and the amount of the alleged loss or damage suffered.
The Master shall provide my/our principal with full details of the alleged default and loss or damage available to the said Master at the time
of making the demand;

(b)   (i)   the Master shall on request afford my/our principal or any representative appointed by it an opportunity of investigating the alleged default and loss or damage, and shall disclose and make available all information and documents in his possession or under his control relative thereto and shall generally co-operate with and assist my/our principal in his investigations to the extent that it is in his power to do so;

       (ii)   my/our principal shall notify the Master in writing, of its objection (if any) to the claim or the amount thereof and the grounds therefor within three months from the date of such notification by the Master or within such further period as the Master may allow in writing having regard to the reasonable requirements of my/our principal for purposes of investigating the alleged default and the amount of the loss or damage so claimed;

(c)   the Master shall notify my/our principal in writing of his decision on any objection lodged by my/our principal to the claim, the validity or amounts thereof and in the event of any rejection of any objection, the grounds therefor;

(d)   in the event and to the extent that the Master shall reject the objections to the claim or the amount thereof, my/our principal shall be entitled to institute action within four months of such rejection;

(e)   the amount paid by my/our principal to the Master in terms of paragraph 1, shall be kept by the Master in trust pending the expiration of the period of four months mentioned in paragraph (d) or the final determination of any action instituted by my/our principal, whichever occurs last.

3.   It is a condition of this bond that if the incumbent(s) shall duly and properly perform his/their duties in relation to the Estate/Company/Trust and the administration of the assets thereof, then the obligation assumed hereunder shall lapse and be of no further force and effect.

4.   I/We on behalf of my/our principal renounce the benefits of excussion anc division with the meaning and effect whereof I/we declare my/our principal to be acquainted.

SIGNED at.. ....on..

            (place)   (date)

AS WITNESSES:

1. ....   1. ....

                                                    for Principal

2. ....   2. ....

                                                    for Principal

SURETYSHIP
by NATURAL PERSONS

I/ we,

1. ....

of. ....

2. ....

of. ....

[Full names, residential and business addresses]

do hereby interpose and bind myself / ourselves as surety / sureties and co-principal debtor(s) in *solidum*, jointly and severally with...

[hereinafter referred to as the Incumbent(s)] unto and in favour of the Master of the High Court

(.. Provincial Division) ("the Master") for the due and proper performance by the Incumbent(s) of his/their duties/functions in the aforesaid office(s) and the proper administration of, and accounting by him/them for all funds and property of the Estate under his/their administration as required by law and in default thereof to pay to the Master on demand an amount up to R..............................

(...rand) as the Master may claim from me / us in respect of such loss or damage as may be suffered by the Estate / Minor(s) / Person under curatorship or any person by reason of such default.

Provided that:

1. My/Our liability hereunder will not exceed the sum of R .... (... rand); and

2. in the event of any alleged default on the part of the incumbent(s) in his / their aforesaid office, giving rise to an alleged claim under this suretyship, I / we will be notified by the Master in writing of the alleged default and the amount of the alleged loss or damage suffered, which notification shall be prima facie proof of such default and the amount of the alleged loss or damage suffered. The Master shall provide me/us with full details of the alleged default and loss or damage available to the said Master at the time of making the demand.
3. I / we agree not to charge any fee for this undertaking.
4. I / we renounce the benefits of excussion and division with the meaning and effect whereof I / we declare myself / ourselves to be acquainted.
5. I / we choose as my / our *domicilium citandi et executandi* and for the purpose of the service of any other notices for the service of any legal process, the following address (not a post box number):

....

....

6. It is a condition of this bond that if the Incumbent(s) shall duly and properly perform his / their duties in relation to the Estate and the administration of the assets thereof, then the obligation assumed hereunder shall lapse and be of no further force and effect.

SIGNED at.. on..
                                    (place)   (date)

AS WITNESSES:

1. ....   1. ....

2. ....   2. ....
                                                                                                      Signature(s)

I regard the above surety/sureties as satisfactory.

Official stamp

....

MAGISTRATE

J294
(81/816066)

REPUBLIC OF SOUTH AFRICA

DEATH NOTICE
(In terms of section 7 of the Administration of Estates Act, 1965)

1. Surname of deceased ....

2. Full first names ....

3. ID/Passport number

4. Population group .... 5. Nationality ....

6. Occupation ....

7. Ordinary place(s) of residence during the 12 months prior to death and the Province(s) ....

8. Date of birth   9. Place of birth ....

10. Date of death

11. Has the deceased left a will? .... 12. Marital status at time of death ....

13. If married, place where married ....

14. Full names of surviving spouse ....

   and his/her ID/Passport number ....

15. State whether marriage was in or out of community of property/whether accrual system is applicable.

....

(a) Name(s) of predeceased spouse(s) and/or divorced spouse(s) (state opposite name of each whether predeceased or divorced)

....

(b) Date of death of predeceased spouse(s) ....

16. Master's office(s) where predeceased's estate(s) is/are registered and number(s) of estate(s), if available

....

17. Full names of children of deceased (state whether major or minor or predeceased and in the latter event, whether they left issue and, if that be the case, the full names of such issue)

....

....

18. Names of parents of deceased (state whether parents alive or deceased):

(a) Father ....

(b) Mother ....

19. Name and address of person signing the death notice ....

20. *Capacity ....

21. (a) Was the signatory present at the deceased's death? ....

(b) If the answer to the previous question is no, did the signatory identify the deceased after his death? ....

Dated at .... the .... day of .... in the year ....

....
Print Name **Signature**

* State whether signatory is surviving spouse, nearest blood relative or connection residing in the district in which death has taken place; or is caused by such spouse, blood relative or connection to give this notice; or is required by the Master to submit this death notice.

‡ If the answer to both questions is no, a death certificate or a certified copy must be submitted herewith.

the doj & cd

Department:
Justice and Constitutional Development
REPUBLIC OF SOUTH AFRICA

AFFIDAVIT/DECLARATION

I,……I,……

Am about to apply to the Master of High Court………………………………………………………………

in the estate of the late …………………………………………………………………………………………

for an appointment as an Executor/Executrix and I hereby affirm/make oath and say:

that to the best of my knowledge and belief that letters of executorships/letters of authority in the estate of the late:

……

have not already been granted by any other Master of High Court or Magistrate in the Republic of South Africa.

Signature of Deponent:……………………………………………………………………………

I certify that before administering the oath/affirmation I have asked the deponent the following questions and wrote his/her answers in his/her presence.

    a. Do you know and understand the contents of the declaration/affidavit?

Answer:................

b. Do you have any objection in taking the prescribed oath/declaration?

Answer:................

c. Do you consider the prescribed oath/declaration as binding on your conscience?

Answer:................

I have satisfied myself as to the identity of the deponent
I certify that the deponent has acknowledged that he/she knows and understands the contents of the declaration.

The above signature/mark of the deponent is affixed to the declaration/affidavit in my presence.

Signed and sworn to/affirmed before me at ....

This .... Day of .... in the year........................

....
Signature of commissioner of oath

Area for which appointed:..

the doj & cd

Department:
Justice and Constitutional Development
REPUBLIC OF SOUTH AFRICA

DECLARATION

I..I......

Declare as Follows

Of (Address) ....Of...

....

1. The deceased (...)

Was well known to me since ....

2. Mark one of the applicable box with an X below:-

☐ I know that the deceased was a single person and that the deceased did not enter into any Customary Union.

☐ I know that the deceased was a widow/widower/divorced person and that the deceased did not enter into Customary Union after his/her marriage was dissolved

- [ ] I know that the deceased was a married person and that the deceased never entered into any Customary Union

- [ ] I know that the deceased was a married person and that the deceased married .... (number) wives in terms of Customary Union

- [ ] I know that the deceased entered into civil marriage and that the deceased also entered into .... (number) Customary Union/s.

This is all I want to declare

SIGNATURE OF DEPONENT ....

Signed and sworn to/affirmed before me at ....

This .... Day of .... in the year...........................

....
Signature of commissioner of oath

Area for which appointed:...

the doj & cd

Department:
Justice and Constitutional Development
REPUBLIC OF SOUTH AFRICA

NOMINATION TO ACT AS EXECUTOR OR MASTER'S REPRESENTATIVE

Estate late: ____

I / We the undersigned hereby nominate/s ____

to act as executor or Master's representative of the above estate.

Name	Relationship / Capacity	Signature	Date

189

SOUTH AFRICAN REVENUE SERVICE

REV 16

Claim for refund out of revenue

SARS branch office

Claim number

Reference number

Notes

1. Refund of spoiled Revenue Stamps must be claimed on form Rev 17
2. Original receipts of pauments made must be attached. If the original receipts (e.g. transfer duty or master's fees) form part of the records of another office, columns 7 and 8 must be carefully completed.
3. If the refund is claimed on behalf of someone else, a power of attorney must be produced.
4. Submit full reasons for the claim for refund, if necessary on a separate sheet or paper.

Part A (To be completed by claimant)

I, (full name of claimant)

Identity number   hereby claim a refund of **R**

for the following reasons

Payments made				Amount which should of been paid	Overpayment now claimed	Officer where original receipt is lodged	Reference number of the record in such office
Office of employment Date 1		Receipt no. 2	Amount 3	4	5	6	7
							8
		Total					

Signature of claimant or authorised representative   Date   Postal address

Part B (To be completed by the collecting office) (Indicate the applicable option with an "X")

1. The original receipt   is attached, or

| | | is attached, or |
| | | is attached, or |

2. The claim is for | | the full amount paid, or

| | part of amount and the receipt has been endorsed

3. To prevent a double refund this claim has been noted in red ink in:

| | Cashbook or Daybook folio number

| | Counterfoil of receipt(s) number(s)

| | Card or loose leaf register

4. The amount claimed above was originally collected as | | State Revenue   or | | Provincial Revenue

and in the Rev 6 the amount was originally allocated to:

5. A cheque for   **R**   ,   is required for an outstanding amount under the head:

6. Certificate: I am satisfied that this refund is due and properly payable

A refund of   **R**   ,   is recommended

Part C (To be completed by authorising officer)

Payee (1)

Address

Payee (2)

Address

Head of Revenue	Amount	Cheque number	Date issued	Received the amount of
				in full settlement of the above claim

Commisioner for SARS | Date

Signature | Date

SARS

ESTATE DUTY
BOEDELBELASTING

REV 246

Valuation of immovable property
Waardering van onroerende eiendom

Notes:
Notas:

1. Any additional information can be submitted as an addendum to this form.
   Enige bykomende inligting kan as 'n aanhangsel tot hierdie vorm verskaf word.
2. The person performing the valuation should retain all supporting documentation (sketches, photographs, etc.), for possible future enquiries.
   Die persoon wat die waardering uitvoer moet alle stawende bewysstukke behou (sketse, fotos, ens.), vir moontlike toekomstige navrae.
3. Delete if not applicable.
   Skrap indien nie van toepassing.
4. A separate form must be used for each property. This form will not be accepted unless completed in full.
   'n Afsonderlike vorm moet vir elke eiendom gebruik word. Die vorm sal verwerp word indien dit nie volledig voltooi is nie.

PART A   Instruction for valuation of immovable property
DEEL A   Opdrag vir waardering van onroerende eiendom

Estate late
Boedel wyle

Estate's number
Boedelnommer

Master's office
Meesterskantoor

ID number of deceased
ID nommer van oorledene

Name of executor
Naam van eksekuteur

Please furnish me as executor / representative of the estate with the fair market value as at date of death
Voorsien my as eksekuteur / verteenwoordiger van die boedel met die billike markwaarde soos op datum van afsterwe

of the following property described in Title Deed No
van die volgende eiendom beskryf in Titelakteno.

as
synde

in extent
in grootte

and (in the case of urban property only) situated at (address)
en (in die geval van stedelike eiendom) geleë te (adres)

The following further particulars are furnished in respect of this property
Die volgende besonderhede betreffende die eiendom word verstrek

1. Registered owner
   Geregistreerde eienaar

2. Date of acquisition
   Datum van verkryging

3. How acquired
   (purchase, inheritance, etc.)
   Hoe verkry
   (aankoop, erflating, ens.)

4. Value at date of acquisition
   Waarde op datum van verkryging   R

5. Amount of bonds registered against the property
   Bedrag van geregistreerde verbande teen die eiendom   R

6. Municipal Valuation
   Munisipale Waardasie

   6.1 Date of such
       municipal valuation
       Datum van muni-
       sipale waardasie

   6.2 Date of implemen-
       tation
       Datum van inwer-
       kingtreding

   6.3 Land value
       Grondwaarde   R

   6.4 Improvements
       Verbeterings   R

   6.5 Total value
       Totale waarde   R

7. Limited interests, eg. usufruct, *fideicommissum*, leasehold rights, servitudes or restrictions (normal township conditions excluded)
   Beperkte belange bv. vruggebruik, *fideicommissum*, erfpagregte, serwitute of beperkings (normale dorpsgebiedbeperkings uitgesluit)

   registered against the property
   teen die eiendom geregistreer

8. Mineral rights
   Mineraalregte

   8.1 Are there mineral rights attached to the property in terms of the Mineral and Petroleum Resources Development Act,
       Act No 28 of 2002. Is daar mineraalregte aan hierdie eiendom verbonde ingevolge die bepalings van die "Mineral and
       Petroleum Resources Development Act, Act No. 28 of 2002"

   8.2 If "Yes", give full details on a separate sheet
       Indien "Ja", verstrek volle besonderhede op 'n aparte vel

9. Other considerations
important to the determi-
nation of the value are
Ander oorwegings be-
langrik by die vasstelling
van die waarde is

Signature Handtekening	Capacity Hoedanigheid	Date Datum

Postal address
Posadres

PART B **Valuation report** - to be completed by Valuer
DEEL B **Waarderingsverslag** - vir voltooiing deur Waardeerder

General information regarding the property
Algemene inligting aangaande die eiendom

At date of death   the property was
Op datum van afsterwe   was die eiendom

1. Occupied by the owner
    Bewoon deur die oorledene

2. Rented out
    Verhuur

2.1 If rented out, submit the amount of rental received per month   R
    Indien uitverhuur, vermeld die huurgeld ontvang per maand

2.2 Submit the market related rental (if the rental as reflected above is not market related)   R
    Voorsien die markverwante huurgeld (indien bogemelde nie 'n markverwante huurgeld is nie)

2.3 Was the property subject to a lease agreement?
    Was die eiendom onderworpe aan 'n verhuringsooreenkoms?

    If "Yes" the following information must be submitted
    Indien "Ja", verstrek asseblief die volgende inligting

    - unexpired lease period   years   months
      onverstreke verhuringstydperk   jaar   maande

- the amount of rental payable per month / annum
  die huurgeld betaalbaar per maand / jaar   R

3. Unoccupied
    Onbewoon

PART C Valuation report - Residential property
DEEL C Waarderingsverslag - Residensiële eiendom

To be completed for urban residential houses, residential sectional title units, agricutural holdings upon which no *bona fide* farming activities are being carried on and small farm portions used exclusively for residential purposes. For vacant land and the above uses the section on comparable transactions in Part F must be completed. If the vacant land has potential for an alternative use, provide motivation with regard to the potential on a seperate sheet.

Moet voltooi word ten opsigte van stedelike residensiële eiendom, residensiële deeltiteleenhede, landbouhoewes waarop daar nie *bona fide* boerdery-bedrywighede plaasvind nie en klein plaasgedeeltes wat uitsluitlik vir residensiële doeleindes gebruik word. Ten opsigte van onbeboude grond en bogenoemde gebruike moet die afdeling ten opsigte van vergelykende transaksies gemeld in Deel F voltooi word. Indien die onbeboude grond potensiaal het vir alternatiewe gebruike, verskaf motivering vir gemelde potensiaal op 'n aparte vel.

Legal property description
or sectional title scheme
Wetlike eiendomsbeskry-   and scheme number
wing of deeltitelskema   en skemanommer

Extent of land / unit
Grootte van eiendom /   ha/m²
eenheid

Describe the area where
the property is situated
Beskryf die gebied waar
die eiendom geleë is

Approximate age of improvements   years
Geskatte ouderdom van verbeterings   jare

Approximate area of improvements
Geskatte oppervlakte van verbeterings

Dwelling 1   ±   m²   Dwelling 2 / Flat / Cottage   ±   m²
Woning 1   Woning 2 / Woonstel / Kothuis

Outbuilding(s) 1 ±   m²   Outbuilding(s) 2   ±   m²
Buitegebou(e) 1   Buitegebou(e) 2

Veranda   ±   m²   Lapa   ±   m²   Carport   ±   m²
Stoep   Lapa   Motorafdak

Other (specify)
Ander (spesifiseer)

	Finishing Afwerking	State of repair Toestand van verbeterings
Roof: Dwelling Dak: Woning		
Outbuilding(s) Buitegebou(e)		
Walls: Exterior Mure: Buiteafwerking		
Interior Binneafwerking		
Floor covering Vloerbedekking		
Ceilings Plafonne		

Facilities offered - Indicate the quantity of each room type
Fasiliteite beskikbaar - Dui die hoeveelhede van elke tipe vertrek aan

Dwelling 1 or Sectional Title Unit Woning 1 of Deeltitel eenheid						Dwelling 2 / Flat / Cottage Woning 2 / Woonstel / Kothuis	
Entrance Hall Ingangsportaal		Kitchen Kombuis		Baths Baddens		Bedrooms Slaapkamers	
Lounge Sitkamer		Laundry Waskamer		Showers Storte		Living rooms Woonkamers	
Dining room Eetkamer		Scullery Opwaskamer		Toilets Toilette		Kitchen Kombuis	
Family room Woonkamer		Pantry Spens				Baths Baddens	
Entertainment area Onthaal area		Bedrooms Slaapkamers				Showers Storte	
Bar Kroeg		Dressing room Aantrekkamer				Toilets Toilette	
Study Studeerkamer							

Outbuilding 1 Buitegebou 1		Outbuilding 2 Buitegebou 2		Carport - under roof Motorafdak - onderdak		Other Ander	
Garages Motorhuise				Steel & IBR Staal & IBR		Alarm system Alarmstelsel	
Room(s) Kamer(s)				Shade net Skadunet		Motorised gate Gemotoriseerde hek	
Showers / Baths Storte / Baddens						Irrigation Besproeiing	
Toilets Toilette							
Stores Store							

Sundries: Indicate type of finishing / equipment Algemeen: Dui aan die tipe afwerking / toerusting	
Fencing Omheining	
Driveway and paving Oprit en plaveisel	
Borehole Boorgat	
Swimming pool Swembad	
Jacuzzi Borrelbad	
Lapa Lapa	
Other (Tennis court, etc.) Ander (Tennisbaan, ens.)	

Fair market value of the property with reference to the transactions in Part F
Billike markwaarde van die eiendom met verwysing na die transaksies in Deel F   R

PART D Valuation report - Farm property
DEEL D Waarderingsverslag - Plaaseiendom

To be completed for farm property. The value of unreaped crops or unpicked fruits, plantations, orchards, vineyards, also planted lucern, sugar cane, pineapples, cotton and the like must be included in this part. If necessary to elaborate, an addendum can be added to this form. Indicate comparable transactions in Part F.

Moet voltooi word vir plaaseiendom. Die waarde van die ongeoeste gewasse, ongeplukte vrugte, plantasies, boorde, wingerde, lusern, suikerriet, pynappels, katoen en enige ander gewasse moet ingesluit word. Indien nodig om uit te brei, kan 'n aanhangsel aangeheg word. Dui vergelykende transaksies aan in Deel F.

Legal property description
Wetlike eiendomsbe-
skrywing

Extent of property
Grootte van eiendom   ha/m²

Location (Indicate nearest main road, distance and direction from nearest large town / city)
Ligging (Dui die naaste hoofpad, afstand en rigting vanaf naaste groot dorp / stad aan)

Type of farming activities
Soort boerdery beoefen

Does the farm have the potential for alternative uses?
Het die plaas potensiaal vir alternatiewe gebruike?

Motivate if 'YES'
Motiveer indien 'JA'

General type of farming in
the area
Algemene soort boerdery
in die omgewing

General topography
Algemene topografie

Stock carrying capacity of grazing   ha per large stock unit   ha per small stock unit
Veedrakrag van weiveld   ha per grootvee-eenheid   ha per kleinvee-eenheid

Approximate area of buildings and state of repair   **Use spaces provided for other buildings**
Benaderde oppervlakte van geboue en toestand daarvan   **Gebruik die spasie voorsien vir ander geboue**

	m²	good / fair / poor goed / redelik / swak		m²	good / fair / poor goed / redelik / swak
Dwelling Woning			Dwelling Woning		
Outbuildings Buitegeboue			Outbuildings Buitegeboue		
Sheds Skure			Sheds Skure		

Describe water sources eg. boreholes, water permit, water listing, etc.
Beskryf die waterbronne bv. boorgate waterkwota, waterpermit, ens.

Notional apportionment of determined market value with reference to comparable transactions in Part F
Berekening van verdeling van markwaarde met verwysing na vergelykende transaksies in Deel F

	Soil type Grond tipe	Ha		R/Ha		Value Waarde
Grazing Weiding			R		R	
Dry land Droëland			R		R	
Irrigable land Besproeibare grond			R		R	
Land under irrigation Grond onder besproeiing			R		R	
Crops under irrigation (eg.citrus, sugar, etc.) Gewasse onder besproeiing (bv. sitrus, suiker, ens.)			R		R	
Other development / uses Ander ontwikkeling / gebruike			R		R	
Sub total **Subtotaal**					R	
Add: Improvements Plus: Verbeterings					R	
Total value as determined Totale waarde soos bepaal					R	
Add: Value of standing crops as at date of death Plus: Waarde van oes op lande soos op datum van afsterwe					R	
TOTAL **TOTAAL**					R	

Capital Gains Tax: Indicate the value of the primary residence and the land on which it is situated as does not exceed two hectares.
Kapitaalwinsbelasting: Dui aan die waarde van die primêre woning tesame met die grond waarop dit geleë is wat nie twee hektaar oorskry nie

R

Confirm whether *bona fide* farming operations are being carried on on the property
Bevestig of *bona fide* boerdery bedrywighede op die grond beoefen word

If "Yes", state reasons why you are of the opinion that *bona fide* farming operations are conducted on the property
Indien "*Ja*", verstrek redes waarom u beweer dat *bona fide* boerdery-bedrywighede op die eiendom beoefen word

PART E Valuation report - Business and related property
DEEL E Waarderingsverslag - Besigheid en verwante eiendom

To be completed for any income producing property eg. shops, offices, flats, industrial property and non-residential sectional title units. For vacant non-residential property and sectional title units, the section on comparable transactions in Part F must be completed.
Moet voltooi word ten opsigte van inkomstelewerende eiendom bv. winkels, kantore, woonstelle, industriële eiendom en nie-residensiële deeltitel-eenhede. Vir onbeboude nie-residensiële eiendom en deeltitel eenhede, moet die afdeling vergelykende transaksies in Deel F voltooi word.

Registered description of property
Geregistreerde beskrywing van eiendom

Extent of property
Grootte van eiendom — ha/m^2

Town planning restrictions Zoning
Dorpsbeplanningsbeperkings Sonering

FSR / VRV Coverage % / Dekking % Height / Hoogte

Current use of property
Huidige gebruik van eiendom

Highest and best use
Voordeligste en beste gebruik

General state of repair of improvements
Algemene toestand van verbeterings

Approximate age of improvements
Geskatte ouderdom van verbeterings — years / jare

Construction type of
improvements
Konstruksietipe van
verbeterings

Describe the general
area where the property
is situated
Beskryf die algemene om-
gewing waar die eiendom
geleë is

Summary of valuation
Opsomming van waardering

(i) Determination of the value of an income producing property
Bepaling van die waarde van 'n inkomstelewerende eiendom

Rentable area of building used for offices, shops or industrial purposes
Verhuurbare oppervlakte van gebou gebruik vir kantore, winkels of industriële doeleindes   m²

Areas for storage   Number of parking bays
Oppervlakte vir stoorarea   m²   Getal parkeerplekke

Potential gross annual income   R
Potensiële bruto jaarlikse inkomste

Less: Potential vacant area   R
Min: Potensiële onbesette oppervlakte

                                              Sub Total   R
                                              Subtotaal

Less: Market related annual operating cost of property   R
Min: Markverwante jaarlikse bedryfskoste van eiendom

                                              Sub Total   R
                                              Subtotaal

Net income   R
Netto inkomste

Capitalised   @   R
Gekapitaliseer

Add: Contributing value of additional developable land (if applicable) R
Plus: Bydraende waarde van addisionele ontwikkelbare grond (indien van toepassing)

                                              Total   R
                                              Totaal

(ii) Value of vacant land or sectional title unit with reference to transactions in Part F   R
     Waarde van onbeboude grond of deeltiteleenheid met verwysing na die transaksies in Deel F

Market value rounded of   R
Markwaarde afgerond

(iii) Are the leases market related?
Is die huurkontrakte markverwant?   If not, motivate variation
Indien nie, motiveer afwyking

PART F Comparable transactions used to substantiate the fair market value
DEEL F Vergelykende transaksies gebruik om die billike markwaarde te bepaal

Transaction 1 / Transaksie 1		Comments on comparability / Kommentaar met betrekking tot vergelykbaarheid
Suburb / Town / Scheme / Farm + Reg division Voorstad / Stad / Skema / Plaas + Reg afdeling		
Erf / Holding / Unit / Farm portion Erf / Hoewe / Eenheid / Plaasgedeelte		
Purchase price Aankoopprys		
Purchase date Datum van aankoop		
Extent of land / unit Grootte van eiendom / eenheid		
R / ha or of R / m^2		

Transaction 2 / Transaksie 2		Comments on comparability / Kommentaar met betrekking tot vergelykbaarheid
Suburb / Town / Scheme / Farm + Reg division Voorstad / Stad / Skema / Plaas + Reg afdeling		
Erf / Holding / Unit / Farm portion Erf / Hoewe / Eenheid / Plaasgedeelte		
Purchase price Aankoopprys		
Purchase date Datum van aankoop		
Extent of land / unit Grootte van eiendom / eenheid		
R / ha or of R / m^2		

Transaction 3 / Transaksie 3		Comments on comparability / Kommentaar met betrekking tot vergelykbaarheid

Suburb / Town / Scheme / Farm + Reg division Voorstad / Stad / Skema / Plaas + Reg afdeling		
Erf / Holding / Unit / Farm portion Erf / Hoewe / Eenheid / Plaasgedeelte		
Purchase price Aankoopprys		
Purchase date Datum van aankoop		
Extent of land / unit Grootte van eiendom / eenheid		
R / ha or of R / m²	123	

PART G   Declaration of value
DEEL G   Verklaring van waarde

I,
Ek,   , Professional Valuer, Professional Associated Valuer,
, Professionele Waardeerder, Professionele Geassosieerde

Appraiser or other (specify)   declare that I have inspected the property
Waardeerder, Taksateur of ander (spesifiseer)   verklaar dat ek die eiendom soos omskryf in

described in Part A and have completed the relevant parts of this form.
Deel A geïnspekteer het en die toepaslike dele van die vorm voltooi het.

The fair market value of the property (including improvements and standing crops) as at: is determined at
Die billike markwaarde van die eiendom (insluitende verbeterings en staande oeste) soos op   is vasgestel op

R   in words
                               in woorde

Business address
Besigheidsadres

Telephone number
Telefoonnommer

Signature
Handtekening

Date
Datum

ESTATE DUTY
BOEDELBELASTING

REV267

Return of information required in terms of section 7 of the Estate Duty Act, Act 45 of 1955

Opgawe van inligting wat ingevolge artikel 7 van die Boedelbelastingwet, Wet 45 van 1955, vereis word

NB. Interest on Estate Duty

Section 10 of the Estate Duty Act, Act 45 of 1955, provides that interest must be paid on the amount of any estate duty which is paid within 30 days of the date of the assessment notice, or, if the assessment is made more than 12 months after the date of death, from a date twelve months after death.

The Commissioner may allow an extension of the time within which payment may be made without interest if a reasonable amount is paid as a deposit against the duty to be assessed and application is made in writing for such extension, provided the deposit is made and the application for extension is lodged before the thirty days period or the twelve month period, as the case may be, has expired.

No formal documentation is required for the payment of a deposit against estate duty at SARS branch offices. (Name, number of estate and date of death must be furnished.)

LW. Rente op Boedelbelasting

Artikel 10 van die Boedelbelastingwet, Wet 45 van 1955, bepaal dat rente betaal moet word op die bedrag van enige boedelbelasting wat nie binne 30 dae vanaf die datum van die aanslagkennisgewing of, indien die aanslag meer as twaalf maande na die datum van dood gehef word, vanaf 'n datum twaalf maande na dood, vereffen is nie.

Die Kommissaris mag 'n verlenging toestaan van die tydperk waarin betaling sonder rente gemaak mag word indien 'n redelike bedrag gestort is as 'n deposito ten opsigte van die belasting wat aangeslaan moet word en skriftelik aansoek gedoen is vir sodanige verlenging, mits die deposito gemaak word en die aansoek om verlenging ingedien word voor die verstryking van die tydperk van dertig dae of die tydperk van twaalf maande, soos die geval mag wees.

Geen formele dokumentasie word vereis vir die betaling van 'n deposito teen boedelbelasting by SARS takkantore nie. (Naam en nommer van boedel en die datum van afsterwe moet verstrek word.)

If there is insufficient space on this form, the information must be submitted on a separate sheet
Indien die spasie op hierdie vorm onvoldoende is, moet die inligting op 'n aparte vel papier verstrek word.

Deceased details
Oorledene se besonderhede

Surname
Van

First name(s)
Voorname

Date of birth
Geboortedatum

Identity number
Identiteitsnommer

Date of death
Datum van dood

Estate number
Boedelnommer

Master's office where estate is reported
Meesterskantoor waar boedel geraporteer is

Last residential address
Laaste woonadres

Postal code
Poskode

Country of ordinary residence
Land waar gewoonlik woonagtig

Period from
Tydperk vanaf

to
tot

If ordinarily resident in a country other than RSA during 10 years immediately preceding the date of death, state name of country and periods resident in that country
Indien binne tien jaar onmiddelik voor datum van dood in 'n ander land as RSA woonagtig, meld naam van land en tydperke aldaar woonagtig

Period from
Tydperk vanaf

to
tot

Details of surviving spouse (if any)
Besonderhede van nagelate gade (indien enige)

Name and Surname
Naam en Van

Address
Adres

Postal code
Poskode

Indicate whether marriage was:
Dui aan of die huwelik

In community of property
Binne gemeenskap van goedere

Out community of property
Buite gemeenskap van goedere

Subject to the accrual system
Onderworpe aan die aanwasbedeling

Place of marriage
Plek van huwelik

Date of marriage
Datum van huwelik

Account 1   - Property of the deceased as at date of death
Rekening 1 - Eiendom van die oorledene soos op datum van dood

A (i) Gross value of all property disclosed in the liquidation and distribution (L&D) account   R
Bruto waarde van alle eiendom in die likwidasie- en distribusierekening (L&D) aangetoon

Deduct: Proceeds of all "domestic policies" of insurance upon the life of the deceased
Min: reflected in the L&D account (sec 3(3)(a))
          Opbrengs van alle "binnelandse assuransiepolisse" op die lewe van die
          oorledene wat in die L&D rekening aangetoon word.   R

          Any benefit which is due and payable by a fund reflected in the L&D account
          (sec 3(3)(a)bis)
          Enige voordeel deur 'n fonds uitbetaal wat in L&D rekening aangetoon word
          (artikel 3(3)(a)bis)   R

          Value of any property which is not "property" as defined in section 3(2)(c)-(h)
          Waarde van enige eiendom wat nie "eiendom" is nie soos in artikel 3(2)(c)-(h)
          omskryf   R

          Selling price of non-listed shares / members interest in CC
          Verkoopsprys van ongenoteerde aandele / ledebelang in BK   R

          Fair market value of farming property as per valuation
          Billike markwaarde van boerdery eiendom per waardasie   R   R   0

Add: Counter-claim for suretyship given by the deceased - if such a claim is included
Plus: in the liabilities reflected in Account 3
          Kontra eis vir borgstelling gegee deur oorledene - indien sodanige eis ingesluit
          is by die laste in Rekening 3   R

          Valuation of non-listed shares / members interest in CC
          Waardasie van ongenoteerde aandele / ledebelang in BK   R

          Fair market value of farming property as per valuation
          Billike markwaarde van boerdery eiendom per waardasie   R

          Less: 30% in terms of (b) of the definition of "fair market
          value"
          Min: 30% in terme van (b) van die wooromskrywing van
          "billike markwaarde"   R   0 R   0 R   0

(Where no L&D account is required to be rendered to any Master of the High Court, a separate statement of all property owned by the deceased at
the date of his/her death should be submitted with this return.)

(Waar dit nie vereis word dat 'n L&D rekening aan 'n Meester van die Hooggeregshof verstrek word nie, moet 'n afsonderlike staat van alle eiendom, deur die oorledene op datum van sy/haar dood besit, saam met hierdie opgawe verstrek word.)

(ii) Value of other property (if any) not reflected in the L&D account:
Waarde van ander eiendom (indien enige) nie in die L&D rekening aangetoon word nie:

(a) Property of which a beneficiary becomes the owner by a nomination agreement entered into by the deceased during his / her lifetime. (See remark 1a on last page)
Eiendom waarvan 'n begunstigde die eienaar word deur middel van 'n nominasie ooreenkoms deur die oorledene gesluit tydens sy / haar leeftyd. (Sien nota 1a op laaste bladsy)
Description of property
Beskrywing van eiendom

Value
Waarde   R

(b) Immovable and movable property situated outside the Republic. (See remark 1b on last page)
Roerende en onroerende eiendom buite die Republiek ge eë. (Sien nota 1b op laaste bladsy)
Description of property and where situated
Beskrywing van eiendom en waar geleë

Value
Waarde   R

(c) Shares held by or on behalf of the deceased in a company (See remark 1c on last page)
Aandele deur of namens die oorledene gehou in 'n maatskappy (Sien nota 1c op laaste bladsy)
Name of company and country of incorporation as well as the number and description of shares held
Naam van maatskappy en land waar geinkorporeer asook die aantal en beskrywing van aandele gehou

Value
Waarde   R

Account 1   - Property of the deceased as at date of death (continued)
Rekening 1 - Eiendom van die oorledene soos op datum van dood (vervolg)

(d) Any debt not recoverable or right of action not enforceable in the courts of the Republic (See remark 1d on last page)
Enige skuld of reg van aksie wat nie in die geregshowe van die Republiek verhaalbaar of afdwingbaar is nie (Sien nota 1d op laaste bladsy)

Name and address of debtor or other institution, etc., liable for payment
Naam en adres van skuldenaar of ander inrigting, ens., wat vir betaling aanspreeklik is

Value
Waarde   R

(e) Gratuities or benefit society awards (See remark 1e on last page)
Gratifikasie of toekenings van 'n onderlinge hulpverening (Sien nota 1e op laaste bladsy)

By whom payable as well as the name and address of person to whom gratuity or reward is payable
Deur wie betaalbaar asook die naam en adres van die persoon aan wie die gratifikasie of toekenning betaalbaar is

Value
Waarde   R

Total of A(i), A(ii), (a), (b), (c), (d) and (e)
Totaal van A(i), A(ii), (a), (b), (c), (d) en (e)   R   0

Less: Survivor's share thereof if the marriage was in community of property
Min: Oorlewende se aandeel indien die huwelik in gemeenskap van goedere was   R

A   R   0

B. Value of any fiduciary, usufructuary or other like interest in property situated in the Republic. Section 3(2)(a) read with section 5(1)(b)
Waarde van enige fidusiêre reg, vruggebruik of ander derglike reg op eiendom in die Republiek geleë. Artikel 3(2)(a) saamgelees met artikel 5(1)(b)

Description of the burdened property
Beskrywing van beswaarde eiendom

Nature of interest, when and how the deceased acquired it.
Aard van reg, hoe en wanneer oorledene dit verkry het.

Fair market value of property at date of death of deceased (except farming property)
Billike markwaarde van eiendom op datum van dood van oorledene (uitgesonderd boerdery eiendom)   R
Fair market value of farming property less 30%
Billike markwaarde van boerdery eiendom min 30%   R

Name, address and date of birth of person who upon the cessation of deceased's interest becomes entitled to the right of enjoyment of the property and period for which such right is held.
Naam, adres en datum van geboorte van persoon wat by verstryking van die oorledene se reg, op die reg van genot van die eiendom geregtig word en die tydperk wat hy/sy die reg sal hou.

Less: Consideration paid for right of ownership and date of payment
Min: Vergoeding betaal vir die eiendomsreg en datum van betaling   R

B   R   0

Account 1   - Property of the deceased as at date of death (continued)
Rekening 1 - Eiendom van die oorledene soos op datum van dood (vervolg)

C. Value of any right to an annuity. (Section 3(2)(b) read with section 5(1)(d))
Waarde van enige reg op 'n jaargeld. (Artikel 3(2)(b) saamgelees met artikel 5(1)(d))

Annual amount of annuity
Jaarlikse bedrag van die jaargeld .... R

How and when deceased first acquired it.
Hoe en wanneer deur oorledene die eerste maal verkry.

Name, address and date of birth of person to whom the annuity accrues on death of deceased and period for which such person is to enjoy the annuity.
Naam, adres en datum van geboorte van persoon aan wie die jaargeld toeval op datum van dood van die oorledene en die periode waarvoor sodanige persoon die jaargeld kan geniet.

Period for which such person is to enjoy the annuity
Tydperk waarvoor sodanige persoon die jaargeld kan geniet ....

Value of interest calculated in terms of paragraph (d) of subsection (1) of section 5 of the Act
Waarde van reg bereken ingevolge paragraaf (d) van subartikel (1) van artikel 5 van die Wet. .... R

Property of the deceased: **Total of A + B + C**
Eiendom van die oorledene: **Totaal van A + B + C**   R   0

Account 2   - Property deemed to be property of the deceased as at the date of death
Rekening 2 - Eiendom wat geag word die eiendom van die oorledene te wees op die datum van dood

A **Proceeds of all 'domestic' policies of insurance upon the life of deceased (Section 3(3)(a))**
   Opbrengs van alle 'binnelandse' assuransiepolisse op die lewe van oorledene (Artikel 3(3)(a))

Name of company Naam van maatskappy	Number of policy Nommer van polis	Name and address of person to whom proceeds are payable Naam en adres van die persoon aan wie die opbrengs betaalbaar is	Gross proceeds of policy Bruto opbrengs van polis

Gross value of all policies
Bruto waarde van alle polisse   R   0

Less: (i) Aggregate amount of premiums paid by the person (other than the deceased) entitled to the proceeds plus interest at 6% per annum
Min: thereon as calculated on a separate sheet.
       Totale bedrag premies betaal deur die persoon (behalwe die oorledene) wat geregtig is op die opbrengs plus rente daarop teen 6%
       per jaar soos bereken op 'n aparte bladsy.

     (ii) Consideration paid by the person entitled to the proceeds plus interest at 6% per annum thereon.
        Vergoeding betaal deur die persoon geregtig op die opbrengs plus rente daarop teen 6% per jaar.

     (iii) Proceeds of policy recoverable by surviving spouse or child of deceased under a registered antenuptial or post nuptial contract.
        Opbrengs van polis verhaalbaar deur die oorlewende eggenoot of kind van die oorledene uit hoofde van 'n regeregistreerde voor- of
        na-huwelikse kontrak.

     (iv) Proceeds of policy taken out or acquired by a partner/co-member of CC/co-shareholder of the deceased as envisaged in section
        3(3)(a)(iA).
        Opbrengs van polis uitgeneem deur 'n vennoot/mede-lid van 'n BK/mede-aandeelhouer van die oorledene kragtens artikel
        3(3)(a)(iA).

     (v) Proceeds of policies which were not effected by or at the instance of the deceased, as envisaged in terms of section 3(3)(a)(ii).
        Opbrengs van polisse wat nie deur of in opdrag van die oorledene uitgeneem is nie, soos omskryf in artikel 3(3)(a)(ii).

Total of (i) - (v)
Totaal van (i) - (v)   R

Net value of all taxable policies
Netto waarde van alle belasbare polisse   R   0

211

Account 2 - Property deemed to be property of the deceased as at the date of death (continued)
Rekening 2 - Eiendom wat geag word die eiendom van die oorledene te wees op die datum van dood (vervolg)

B   Benefit due and payable from a fund: (Section 3(3)(a)bis)
Voordeel uit fonds verskuldig en betaalbaar: (Artikel 3(3)(a)bis)

Name of fund
Naam van fonds

Name and address of the person to whom payable
Naam en adres van die persoon aan wie betaalbaar

Less: Contributions or consideration paid by the beneficiary together with 6% interest.
Min: Bydraes of vergoeding betaal deur die begunstigde tesame met 6% rente .... R

Net benefit due and payable by any fund
Netto voordeel verskuldig en betaalbaar deur enige fonds .... R

C   Value of property donated in terms of section 56(1)(c) or (d) of the Income Tax Act, if not otherwise included as property of the deceased for purposes of this Act. (Section 3(3)(b))
Waarde van eiendom geskenk ingevolge artikel 56(1)(c) of (d) van die Inkomstebelastingwet, indien nie andersins ingesluit as eiendom van die oorledene, vir doeleindes van hierdie Wet. (Artikel 3(3)(b))

Description of property
Beskrywing van eiendom

Name and address of the person benefiting
Naam en adres van die bevoordeelde persoon

Value
Waarde .... R

D **Property acquired by the deceased under section 3 of the Matrimonial Property Act, 1984, in respect of any accrual contemplated in that section: (Section 3(3)(cA))**
Eiendom verkry deur die oorledene kragtens artikel 3 van die Wet op Huweliksgoedere, 1984, ten opsigte van enige toevalling in daardie artikel: (Artikel 3(3)(cA))

Name and address of deceased's spouse or, if deceased, name and address of executor, estate's number and Master's office where reported.
Naam en adres van die oorledene se gade of, indien oorlede, die naam en adres van die eksekuteur, boedelnommer en Meesterskantoor waar boedel gerapporteer is

Amount of claim
Bedrag van eis   R

E **Property, meaning property situated where ever (i.e. property which has not already been accounted for in this return) of which the deceased was immediately prior to his death competent to dispose of for his own benefit or the benefit of his estate (Section 3(3)(d) read with Section 3(5))**
Eiendom, met inbegrip van eiendom waar ook al geleë (dws. eiendom nie voorheen in hierdie opgawe verantwoord nie) waaroor die oorledene onmiddellik voor sy dood bevoeg was om vir sy eie voordeel of vir die voordeel van sy boedel te beskik (Artikel 3(3)(d) saamgelees met Artikel 3(5))

Description of property
Beskrywing van eiendom

Person in whose name registered
Persoon in wie se naam geregistreer

Value
Waarde   R

Total of A + B + C + D + E
Totaal van A + B + C + D + E   R   0

Account 3   - Deductions claimed in terms of section 4 of the Act
Rekening 3 - Kortings geëis ingevolge artikel 4 van die Wet

A Total amount of liabilities disclosed in the L&D account (where no L&D account is required to be rendered to any Master of the High Court a separate statement of liabilities should be submitted with this return)
Totale bedrag laste soos in die L&D rekening aangetoon (waar dit nie vereis word dat 'n L&D rekening aan 'n Meester verstrek word nie moet 'n afsonderlike staat van laste met hierdie opgawe verstrek word).   R

Less: Any claim to property donated by the deceased in terms of section 56(1)(c) or (d) of the Income Tax Act included in the total amount of liabilities
Min: Eiendom geskenk deur die oorledene ingevolge artikel 56(1)(c) of (d) van die Inkomste-belastingwet ingesluit in die totale bedrag laste   R

Total A
Totaal A   R   0

B The calculation hereunder only applies where the deceased was married in community of property
Die ondergemelde berekening is slegs van toepassing indien die oorledene binne gemeenskap van goedere getroud was

Total A
Totaal A   R   0

Less: Funeral costs
Min: Begrafniskoste   R

½ share of liabilities (excluding funeral costs)
½ aandeel van die laste (uitgesluit begrafniskoste)   R   R   0

Add: Funeral costs - where the deceased was married in community of property
Plus: Begrafniskoste - waar oorledene binne gemeenskap van goedere getroud was   R

Total B
Totaal B   R   0

Total A **or** B
Totaal A **of** B .... R

Add: Deduction claimed in terms of:
Plus: Korting geëis ingevolge:

Section 4(e) deduction (If the deceased was married in community of property claim
only ½ share of the value of the said property)
Artikel 4(e) aftrekking (Indien oorledene binne gemeenskap van goedere getroud was,
eis slegs ½ van die waarde van die betrokke eiendom) .... R

Section 4(f)
Artikel 4(f) .... R

Section 4(g)
Artikel 4(g) .... R

Section 4(h)
Artikel 4(h) .... R

Section 4(i) & (j)
Artikel 4(i) & (j) .... R

Section 4(m)
Artikel 4(m) .... R

Section 4(o)
Artikel 4(o) .... R

Section 4(p)
Artikel 4(p) .... R

Section 4(q)
Artikel 4(q) .... R   R   0

Total deductions claimed
Totale kortings geëis .... R   0

Summary
Opsomming

Account 1 - Value of all property of the deceased
Rekening 1 - Waarde van alle eiedom van die oorledene   R   0

Account 2 - Value of all property deemed to be property of the deceased
Rekening 2 - Waarde van alle eiendom wat geag word eiendom van die oorledene te wees   R   0   R   0

Less: Account 3 - Deductions claimed in terms of section 4 of the Act
Min: Rekening 3 - Aftrekkings geeis ingevolge artikel 4 van die Wet   R   0

Net value of estate
Netto waarde van boedel   R   0

Less: Section 4A
Min: Artikel 4A   R

Dutiable amount
Belasbare bedrag   R   0

Estate duty payable @   %
Boedelbelasting betaalbaar @   R

Interest on Estate Duty - see section 10 of the Act
Rente op Boedelbelasting - sien artikel 10 van die Wet   R

Details of executor/executrix
Besonderhede van eksekuteur/eksekutrise

Name
Naam

Address
Adres

Postal code
Poskode

Name
Naam

Address
Adres

Postal code
Poskode

Details of agent
Besonderhede van agent

Name
Naam

Address
Adres

Postal code
Poskode

Declaration by executor(s)
Verklaring deur eksekuteur(s)

I/We, the aforesaid executor(s), hereby certify that the particulars stated in this return are true and correct to the best of my/our knowledge and belief, and that, having made due and diligent enquiry, I/we are not aware of any other property which should be included in the return.
Ek/Ons, die voormelde eksekuteur(s), verklaar dat die besonderhede in hierdie opgaaf uiteengesit juis en waar is na my/ons beste kennis en wete, en dat, nadat ons behoorlik en deeglik ondersoek gedoen het, ek/ons nie bewus is van enige ander eiendom wat daarby ingesluit moet word nie.

Name of executor(s)   **Signature(s) of executor(s)**
Naam van eksekuteur(s)   **Handtekening(e) van eksekuteur(s)**

Signed at   on this   day of   **20**
Geteken te   op hierdie   dag van

1. Value of other property
Waarde van ander eiendom

(a) Certain investments are structured to grant the owner an option either to transfer the investment into the name of the deceased estate or to be redeemed in full at the request of the executor (in which case it constitutes "property of the deceased") or in the event of a beneficiary being nominated, to be paid to the nominated beneficiary, in which case the value of the investment as at date of death of the deceased must be reflected in the space provided for. The investment can also consist of a "policy" (excluding a "domestic policy on the life of the deceased") which does not mature or pay out on the death of the deceased (owner). Such policies run for an agreed time and can be terminated at the request of the owner.

Sekere beleggings is so saamgestel dat die eienaar daarvan die keuse het dat die belegging by sy / haar boedel of op versoek van die eksekuteur opgevra word (in welke geval dit "eiendom van die oorledene" verteenwoordig) of in die geval waar 'n begunstigde (genomineerde) benoem is gedurende die oorledene se leeftyd, die opbrengs aan die genomineerde uitbetaal word, in welke geval die waarde van die belegging soos op datum van afsterwe verantwoord moet word in die gemelde spasie. Sodanige belegging kan ook bestaan uit 'n "polis" (uitgesonderd 'n "binnelandse polis op die lewe van die oorledene") wat nie opeisbaar of uitbetaal word op datum van afsterwe van die oorledene (eienaar) nie. Sodanige polisse het 'n ooreengekome leeftyd wat beeindig word op versoek van die eienaar.

(b) Movable and immovable property situated outside the Republic (to be completed only in cases in which the deceased was ordinarily resident in the Republic).

Roerende en onroerende eiendom buite die Republiek geleë (voltooi slegs in gevalle waar die oorledene sy gewone verblyfplek in die Republiek gehad het)

(c) Shares held by or for the deceased in a company which, although not incorporated or registered under any law in force in the Republic, carries on business or has an office or place of business or maintains a share transfer register in the Republic, and, in additional, in the case of a deceased person who was ordinarily resident in the Republic at the date of his death, shares held by or for him in any company whatsoever.

Aandele deur of namens die oorledene gehou in 'n maatskappy wat, alhoewel nie geinkorporeer of geregistreer ingevolge 'n Wet wat in die Republiek van krag is nie, in die Republiek besigheid doen of 'n kantoor of 'n besigheidsplek het of 'n aandeleregister in die Republiek in stand hou, en daarbenewens, in die geval van 'n oorledene wat op datum van dood sy gewone verblyfplek in die Republiek gehad het, aandele deur of namens hom gehou in enige maatskappy hoegenaamd.

(d) Any debt not recoverable or right or action not enforceable in the courts of the Republic, including credits at any bank, building society, corporation, trust, etc., outside the Republic (to be completed only in cases in which the deceased was ordinarily resident in the Republic).

Enige skuld of reg van aksie wat nie in die geregshowe van die Republiek verhaalbaar of afdwingbaar is nie, met inbegrip van bedrae wat op krediet van die oorledene staan by enige bank, bougenootskap, maatskappy, trust ens., buite die Republiek (moet slegs ingevul word in gevalle waar die oorledene sy gewone verblyfplek in die Republiek gehad het).

(e) Gratuities or benefit society awards in respect of which the deceased or his estate has a right of action enforceable in the courts of the Republic, and, in additional, in the case of a deceased who was ordinarily resident in the Republic at the date of his death, gratuities or benefit society awards, etc., the rights of action in correction with which are enforceable outside the Republic.

Gratifikasies of toekenings van 'n onderlinge hulpvereniging ten opsigte waarvan die reg van aksie buite die Republiek afdwingbaar is. In die geval van gratifikasies betaalbaar kragtens enige Wet, vermeld die Wet of magtiging waar kragtens toegestaan.

2. **Value of any fiduciary, usufructuary or other like interest in property situated in the Republic** (including a right to an annuity charged upon such property) held by the deceases immediately prior to his death, and, in addition, in the case of a deceased who was ordinarily resident in the Republic at the date of his death, the value of any such interest held in property situated outside the Republic.
   Waarde van enigefidusiëre reg, vruggebruik of ander dergelike reg op eiendom in die Republiek geleë (Met inbegrip van 'n reg op 'n jaargeld waarmee sodanige goed beswaar is) wat die oorledene onmiddelik voor sy dood besit het, en daarbenewens, in die geval van 'n oorledene wat op datum van dood sy gewone verblyfplek in die Republiek gehad het, die waarde van enige sodanige belang in eiendom wat buite die Republiek geleë is.

3. **Value of any right to an annuity** (other than a right to an annuity charged upon property) enjoyed by the deceases immediately prior to his death which accrued to some other person on his death.
   Waarde van enige reg op 'n jaargeld (behalwe 'n reg op 'n jaargeld waarmee enige goed beswaar is) wat die oorledene onmiddelik voor sy dood besit het en wat by sy dood aan iemand anders toeval.

4. If this form is completed in respect of a date prior to 16 March 1988, the names and addresses of the children of the deceased that survive him (stepchildren excluded) and also the names of children of the deceased who predeceased the deceased leaving issue or a spouse surviving the deceased who had not remarried on or before the date of death of the deceased (stepchildren excluded) must be mentioned.
   Indien hierdie vorm voltooi word ten opsigte van 'n datum voor 16 Maart 1988 moet die name en die adresse van kinders van die oorledene wat hom/haar oorleef (stiefkinders uitgesluit) asook die name van kinders van die oorledene wat voor hom te sterwe gekom het en wat nakomelinge nagelaat het wat die oorledene oorleef, of 'n eggenoot nagelaat het wat die oorledene oorleef en wie nie op of voor die datum van afsterwe van die oorledene hertrou het nie, vermeld word.

5. **Penalties:**
   Any person who, after having been called upon to do so by the Commissioner in terms of section 7 of the Act, fails within the period prescribed by the Commissioner, to submit the return required to be submitted in terms of that section or knowingly omits from such return any particulars by the Act to be included therein, shall be guilty of an offence and liable on conviction to a fine or to imprisonment for a period not exceeding two years. In terms of section 28A of the Act, the Commissioner has the power to publish in the *Government Gazette* the names and particulars of the persons who have been convicted of any offence in terms of section 28 and the common law, where the criminal conduct corresponds materially with an offence referred to in section 28 of the Act.
   Strafbepalings:
   Iemand wat, nadat hy/sy kragtens artikel 7 van die Wet, deur die Kommissaris daartoe aangesê is, versuim om binne die voorgeskrewe tydperk die opgawe voor te lê wat volgens daardie artikel voorgelê moet word of wetens besonderhede wat volgens Wet daarin vertstrek moet word, so 'n opgawe weglaat, is aan 'n misdryf skuldig en by skuldigbevinding strafbaar met 'n boete of met gevangenisstraf vir 'n tydperk van hoogtens twee jaar. Die Kommissaris het kragtens die bepalings van artikel 28A van die Wet die bevoegdeheid om die name en besonderhede van die persone wat skuldig bevind word aan 'n misdryf ingevolge artikel 28 van die Wet en die gemenereg, waar die strafbare gedrag wesenlik ooreenstem met die misdryf in artikel 28 van die Wet, in die *Staatskoerant* te publiseer.

ESTATE DUTY
BOEDELBELASTING

REV268

Return of claims paid under policies of insurance which are "Domestic policies" upon the life of a deceased person - Act 45 of 1955 (the Act)

Opgawe van eise uitbetaal ingevolge assuransie-polisse wat "Binnelandse polisse" op lewe van 'n bestorwe persoon is - Wet 45 van 1955 (die Wet)

Information regarding:
Inligting betreffende:

Estate late
Boedel wyle

Identity number
Identiteitsnommer

Date of death
Datum van afsterwe

Last address
Laaste adres

Master's office to which estate was reported
Meester se kantoor waar die boedel gerapporteer is

Master's estate number
Meester se boedelnommer

Name of executor
Naam van eksekuteur

Address of executor
Adres van eksekuteur

Particulars of claims paid:
Besonderhede van eise uitbetaal:

Policy number Polisnommer	Gross proceeds Bruto opbrengs	Annual premium Jaarlikse premie	Name and address of person to whom the proceeds were paid. (If not paid to estate state reason, e.g. cession, nomination, etc.) Naam en adres van die persoon aan wie die opbrengs betaal is. (Indien nie aan boedel betaal nie meld rede, bv. sessie, nominasie, ens.)

In pursuance of the provisions of section 23 of the Act I forward herewth form(s) Rev 268 giving
particulars of all claims paid which in the aggregate amount to not less than R 100 000 in respect of any
one person made by my company under policies of insurance which are 'domestc policies' upon levies of
deceased persons during the quarter ended
Ingevolge die bepalings van artikel 23 van die Wet stuur ek hiermee vorm(s) Rev268 wat besonderhede
bevat van uitbetalings van alle eise wat in totaal nie minder as R 100 000 bedra nie ten opsigte van elke
afsonderlike persoon wat ingevolge assuransiepolisse, wat 'binnelandse polisse' op die lewens van
afgestorwe persone is, deur my maatskappy uitbetaal is gedurende die kwartaal geëindig

Particulars of claims paid:
Besonderhede van eise uitbetaal:

Name of insurer
Naam van versekeraar
Address
Adres

Date
Datum